Israel's New Disciples

Julia Fisher is a writer and radio broadcaster, with a particular interest in investigating true life stories with a supernatural element.

During the past ten years she has travelled frequently to Israel and the Palestinian Authority areas, and taken a deep interest in the growing number of both Jewish and Arab believers in Jesus, reporting on those who are truly reconciled despite the politics of the region, and who are actively working together.

In *Israel's New Disciples* she asks: why are so many Jewish people living in Israel becoming believers in Jesus? Who are they? How do they relate to what the Bible says concerning Israel's role in the nations of the world in being a light for the Gentiles?

From Israel in particular, but also from other countries around the world, a number of Jewish believers are emerging (Messianic Jews) who are passionate, fearless evangelists. The stories in this book feature some of those who are turning their attention to the Arab world in particular. When you consider that no Jewish person is even allowed to travel to many Arab countries, because their safety cannot be guaranteed, this is amazing. So what is happening? How are these people going about their 'mission', and why are they so passionate to share their faith in the God of Israel with the rest of the world?

Israel's
New Disciples

Why are so many Jews turning to Jesus?

Julia Fisher

MONARCH
BOOKS

Oxford, UK & Grand Rapids, Michigan, USA

First published in the UK in 2008 by Monarch Books
(a publishing imprint of Lion Hudson plc),
Wilkinson House, Jordan Hill Road, Oxford OX2 8DR.
Tel: +44 (0)1865 302750 Fax: +44 (0)1865 302757
Email: monarch@lionhudson.com
www.lionhudson.com

ISBN: 978-1-85424-862-6 (UK)
ISBN: 978-0-8254-6194-1 (USA)

Distributed by:
UK: Marston Book Services Ltd, PO Box 269,
Abingdon, Oxon OX14 4YN;
USA: Kregel Publications, PO Box 2607,
Grand Rapids, Michigan 49501

This book is dedicated to all who pray for the peace of Jerusalem.

Contents

Acknowledgments

This book would not have been possible without the co-operation of everybody mentioned herein because this is not 'my' book; rather it is theirs. So my heartfelt thanks to Yoel and Adel Ben David, Ari and Shira Sorko-Ram, David and Lisa Loden, Claude Ezagouri, Daniel Yahav, Evan and Maala Thomas, Arie Bar David, Howard Bass, Arthur and Zellah Goldberg, Eitan Shishkoff, Zvi Randelman, Marcel and Regula Rebiai, Dan Sered and Rita Tsukahira.

Thankyou as well to my publishers Tony Collins and Simon Cox who have worked beyond the call of duty to produce this book.

Foreword

God will fulfil His purposes for His people Israel. The Scriptures are very clear about this, and He is faithful to His Word.

A veil has been over Israel while the harvest among the Gentile nations is being gathered for the Kingdom of God. In due time that veil will be taken away and there will be a sovereign move of God's Spirit among the Jews before Jesus comes again.

Are we beginning to see the first signs of the lifting of that veil? In the past decade there has been a marked increase in the number of Jews in Israel who are meeting with Jesus (Y'shua in Hebrew) Christ as their Messiah.

The biblical evidence is clear that Jesus is the Christ, the Messiah. Now centuries of prejudice and spiritual blindness are giving way to a wonderful and exciting revelation of the truth. In this book Julia Fisher brings together a series of testimonies that are all the more exciting because they are of Jewish believers whose lives have been transformed in Israel by Y'shua, the Messiah, crucified and risen from the dead.

Their journeys of faith have not been easy, for they live in the midst of much deeply felt antagonism towards Y'shua, especially among the orthodox community. These believers have had to face the rejection and even hatred about which He warned His followers.

Here are the stories of men and women who have persevered in their faith against all the odds. Here is the evidence of the amazing grace of God that has sustained them. And here are the first evidences of the exciting years ahead when not only will many more Jews find a personal relationship with their Messiah, but they will also discover their unity with Arabs and other Gentile believers in the same Lord and Saviour.

Julia Fisher has allowed each believer to speak for himself or herself, with no more comment from her than is necessary. I trust that reading these testimonies will stimulate you to pray for the outworking of God's people in Israel, and that you will have the opportunity to visit the land, not only to see the sights, but to see what God is doing among the people there.

Colin Urquhart,
Kingdom Faith Ministries

Introduction

Israel has a destiny that is determined by God and utterly unique. No other nation has the same destiny as Israel, and Israel is the only nation to whom God said, 'I have made you a light for the Gentiles, that you may bring salvation to the ends of the earth.'[1] Is this why the Bible describes Israel as God's 'chosen' people, selected to serve a specific purpose and carry out a particular task?

However, many people (including many Christians) take the view that, by her very existence, Israel is the cause of so much tension and trouble that she could never bring light into the world or salvation to the ends of the earth.

Through the stories of fourteen Messianic Jewish believers living in Israel today, this book explores the evidence which shows that a movement is emerging from within modern Israel; a movement that is gathering pace and will soon be noticed not only by Israelis, but also the rest of the world, proving that Israel is indeed beginning to see her final destiny being fulfilled.

All the interviews were recorded in a two-week period during September 2007 (apart from one which, due to unforeseen circumstances, had to be recorded three weeks later), in order to reveal what was going on at a particular moment in history. There are many other people whose stories are not included in this book as they were not in Israel at the time; if it had been possible to interview them, their stories would simply have added to the weight of evidence.

And so *Israel's New Disciples* reveals a new

phenomenon – Jewish believers in Jesus (Y'shua) who not only understand that the nation of Israel will one day become a 'light for the Gentiles', but who are driven by this vision and are working full time to see it realized.

Much has been written about the Holocaust; that ugly, evil period in European history cannot be excused. However, in 1948, a few years after this particularly dark cloud had passed, a miracle of rebirth occurred as Israel once again rose from the ashes to become a sovereign state.

Fifty years later, in 1998, I visited Yad Vashem, the Holocaust Memorial in Jerusalem. I went on my own. It is not an easy place to visit, and when I eventually emerged into the sunlight, I sat on a wall overlooking modern Jerusalem and realized that whilst thousands of Jewish people had come to live in Israel since the end of the Second World War, the battle was now on for the 'soul' of this battered nation if they were ever going to achieve what God has destined for them, 'to be a light to the Gentiles and bring salvation to the ends of the earth.' They had physically returned to the land but now there had to be a spiritual rebirth if they were to fully realize their destiny. And that's what this book is about.

Previously I have written about reconciliation between Jewish and Arab believers in *Israel: the Mystery of Peace*, and then in *Future for Israel?* I have written about Arab Christians in Israel and the wider Middle East who understand God's plan for Israel and the Jewish people and who are actively praying and working for their salvation. This book tells the stories of an emerging group of Jewish believers – all outspoken evangelists – who have realized that their job, their destiny, is to 'be a light to the Gentiles and bring salvation to the ends of the earth'.

Why are they prepared to share their stories when it is certainly not popular, and can even be dangerous, to be a Jewish believer in Jesus in Israel? And they are certainly not welcome in Islamic countries – no Jew can travel freely in such places. So who are these Jewish believers, where have they come from, why are they so passionate and how are they going about their 'mission'?

Just as many of the Arab Christians I wrote about in *Future for Israel?* were prepared to risk much and 'go public', so many of the people who share their stories in this book are risking much.

However, the facts are that from Israel in particular, as well as other countries around the world, a number of Jewish believers (Messianic Jews) are emerging who are passionate, fearless evangelists. Over the past ten years I have visited Israel on average three or four times a year, researching stories, broadcasting and leading tours. Ten years ago there were only a few hundred Jewish believers in Israel – today there are over 10,000 and their numbers are steadily growing. In a country of only 6 million people, this represents a sizeable increase and the trend is clear.

So what has this got to do with the church in the nations? Avi Snyder, a Jewish evangelist currently working with Jews for Jesus in Germany, says:

> If you love Israel and the Jewish people,
> then understand we were chosen to be a
> light to the nations. The best way for the
> church to interfere with the process of
> world evangelization is to keep the gospel
> away from us Jews, and not to pray for the
> salvation of Israel, and not to pray for the
> people who bring the gospel to the Jewish

people, and believe the lie that Jews don't
need Jesus (Y'shua) to be saved.

But give us the gospel and pray for
the salvation of Israel and pray for those of
us who bring the gospel to our people, and
we'll bring the gospel to everybody we meet,
because that's why we were created!

The stories told in this book feature some of those who
are turning their attention to the nations, even the Arab
world. When you consider that no Jewish person is even
allowed to travel to many Arab countries, because their
safety cannot be guaranteed, this is amazing.

So what is happening? Who are these people? How
are they going about their 'mission' and why are they so
passionate to share their faith?

Julia Fisher,
February 2008

CHAPTER 1

Yoel Ben David

I knew that within half an hour of my touching down at Ben Gurion Airport, this book would begin. And sure enough, it did. There to meet me was Yoel Ben David. I'd never met him before but I recognized him immediately because of the T-shirt he was wearing. I don't know many people who would be comfortable wearing a 'Jews for Jesus' T-shirt at Ben Gurion Airport! But, as I filed through customs and out into the arrivals lounge along with my fellow passengers – many of whom were orthodox Jews dressed in their sombre black habits – there he was!

'Welcome,' he said, 'good to meet you.'

Before leaving England I had spent many weeks researching the right people to interview for this book. They had to fit certain criteria. They had firstly to be Jewish believers. They had to be the 'movers and shakers', the key people God is using in Israel today; the very people who are fulfilling Israel's destiny to be a nation of believers in Jesus, who will cause the nations of the world to realize that the God of Israel, the God of Abraham, Isaac and Jacob is the one true God. I knew that the number of Messianic believers had been steadily growing from only a handful in the 1960s to several thousands today. Could this steady rise in numbers have been accompanied by a steady rise in boldness? I could not have imagined that even ten years ago any Messianic believer would have dared to wear a 'Jews for Jesus' T-shirt so openly in such a public place in Israel.

Yoel led the way to his car, and we drove to a suburb of Tel Aviv called Petah Tiqwa where he lives in a flat with his wife Adel and their three young children. Such was the generosity of this family, that when they heard I was travelling alone, they offered to meet me at the airport and take me to their home for a meal before driving me to my hotel later that evening.

I arrived on a Friday afternoon, and in Israel, sundown on Friday signals the start of *Shabbat*. Whether secular or religious, it seems most Jewish people welcome the start of *Shabbat*. People go home. The roads are quiet. Families gather together for the *Shabbat* meal. This is a custom that is as old as Judaism; a custom that has withstood the onslaught of secularism.

I was greeted by two of Yoel and Adel's three young children; the youngest was only a few weeks old. They had been watching *Mary Poppins* on DVD whilst Adel had been preparing the evening meal. But soon they were showing me their paddling pool on the roof, and as we looked out across the skyline of Tel Aviv, they pointed out various landmarks and the Judean hills in the distance. Across the road, sitting on their balcony, I could see an elderly couple sitting quietly together... waiting. Gradually, as the sun set and darkness fell, I noticed the quietness. There was no sound of traffic. I watched men in the street below making their way to the local synagogue, some hand in hand with their young sons. They were walking fast, almost running, eager to get there; perhaps they were late!

We gathered around the table. Yoel prayed. He took a plaited loaf of bread (the *hallah*) and broke it, and we shared it together, each breaking off a piece before passing it to the next person. Three-year-old Boaz passed me the bread after breaking off a large piece for himself – he was obviously hungry! Yoel poured the wine. It all seemed so natural and a long way removed from the rather 'religious' way we often share the bread and wine together in our communion services in the West. We enjoyed a delicious meal together and the conversation switched from English to German with a sprinkling of Hebrew; Adel, whose parents were originally from Russia, is fluent in Russian, German, English and Hebrew. Yoel also speaks fluent French. The children switched effortlessly between these various languages. Such is the richness of Israeli life – a people drawn from the nations speaking many languages, now merging into one people with one language.

After dinner, when the children were in bed, Yoel and Adel told me their story. Today Yoel is an evangelist based in the Tel Aviv office of Jews for Jesus. He describes himself as a 'missionary', 'doing what a Jews for Jesus missionary does'. He's worked for the organization for just over three years. Part of that time was spent working in New York where he co-led the recent 'Behold Your God' campaign amongst the Hasidic Jews living there. (This evangelistic campaign, which took seven years to complete, was repeated in every city around the world having a population of at least 25,000 Jewish people.) Now both aged twenty-eight, Yoel and Adel married when they were twenty. 'We came to the Lord together,' they said.

'I was born in Israel and lived here for the first three

years of my life,' Yoel began. 'My father worked for a hotel chain, so we spent a year in the Caribbean, followed by ten years in England and three years in Paris. I then went back to England for two years and lived with my grandparents whilst studying for my "A" Levels, and then came back to Israel.' As a result, Yoel speaks Hebrew, English and French fluently. 'My mother is a proud Moroccan Jew, my father is Scottish.'

So did he feel Jewish as a young boy?

'Yes, I certainly did. My Mum ruled the house with her character! So whilst my Dad was happy to have his football on a Saturday and his paper on a Sunday, my Mum was very forceful with our Jewishness. As a result, by the time my brother and I had reached our late teens, we were tired of it. Every time there was anything about Israel on the television, or anything about anyone Jewish, we were made aware of it!

'We were a traditional Jewish family rather than religious. We would sit down every Friday night and because my Dad was not Jewish and I was the elder son, I would say the *Kiddush* [the grace]. We would eat our meal and then, like every other family, we'd go into the living-room, turn on the telly and watch whatever series or funny programme was on. So the fact that I was Jewish was impressed upon me.

'So where did God feature in my life? From the youngest possible age I knew that God existed and I believed that he had something he wanted me to do. Where did Israel feature? Israel was where I was born. Israel was my country. Israel was the land my Mum fought for – she was part of the IDF [the Israeli Defence Force] during the Yom Kippur struggle. She remembered the great days between the Six Day War and the Yom Kippur

War when Israel felt invincible. And until 1993, when my family went through a financial crash, we came to Israel every year.'

Adel's background however, was quite different from Yoel's. Her parents were from Latvia and in 1978 moved to Berlin, where Adel was born.

'I was brought up in a Russian culture – Russian food, Russian music, and Russian language – whilst living in Berlin. My mother died when I was very young, so my grandmother brought me up, and I can remember asking her, "Am I German or am I Russian?" And she would answer me, "You're Jewish!" As a child I couldn't understand that. What category did that belong to? On holy days we would go to the synagogue; but it was more of a social event than religious observance for us – we went because we were Jewish.

'And so I lived in Berlin until I was nineteen. Then I came to Israel and immediately met Yoel at the *ulpan* [language school] at the immigration absorption centre in Ashkelon, and a year later we were married! At that time I was involved in New Age philosophy. Yoel, although he'd had a more traditional Jewish upbringing, wasn't a practising Jew. What connected us in those early days was philosophizing about God. His lifestyle was exactly the opposite of mine. He would smoke – not the right stuff. And he would drink far too much beer. He was cooler than I was! I was a health freak. Within the New Age scene you have two distinct groups of people – those who smoke, and health freaks! Eventually Yoel began to feel convicted about Judaism and rather than keep talking about God, he decided we should do something about it. And that changed everything. He dived in!'

Such was the intensity of their search for God at that

time, Yoel and Adel assumed the lifestyle and dress of the Hasidic Breslov movement connected to Rabbi Neumann.

'In my teenage years I wanted to find out more about God, so I started reading,' Yoel continued. 'I went to the vicar at the school in England and asked him to give me some books about God, including the Koran and some Hindu writings. The real shock for me was that he didn't try to dissuade me or tell me the gospel. As I was reading the Koran on my bed, I remember putting the book down, and the thought came to me that if God exists, I shouldn't really need to read these books. Rather, He should just show up.

'So I said, "God, if you're real, show up." And before me I saw the face of Jesus! I looked at it and I felt a presence in my room; and I felt afraid. I saw a clear vision of God – and ignored it. I decided it was a figment of my imagination. I put it down to the fact that I was living in a Christian culture, and so something had affected my thinking. And I decided to put the whole experience out of my mind.

'When I came to Israel and met Adel, we started discussing and philosophizing about God. We now realize we knew nothing, but at the time we were very intense and really searching to find the truth. Eventually we decided that if we believed in God, we were being hypocritical if we didn't do something about it. I suppose it started out as a sort of experiment. We began observing *Shabbat*. I would study the *Torah* and other writings through the night. We became more *Haredi* (orthadox). We left the language school. We were living together, so gradually the idea of doing that and not being married seemed wrong. We were therefore faced with a choice: separate or get married. We knew we were right for each other, so why wait?'

Yoel and Adel described how, for one and a half years, they attempted to live a 'religious' life. They persevered and they struggled. They changed their dress to look religious. Yoel wore a big *kippah* (skull cap) and a *tsitsit* (prayer tassels) and grew the *peot* (ear-locks).

But, despite their best efforts, they both knew deep down that they had not found what they were searching for, whatever that was. Adel described her feelings of emptiness: 'I felt I hadn't found what I was looking for. Something was wrong. I thought that if I could find a combination of New Age and Judaism, my search would be over.

'However, everything changed when we met Judy. An elderly lady from Richmond, Virginia, she was the aunt of a friend we knew from the absorption centre, and when we moved to Jerusalem we found we lived within walking distance of her. We invited her over and she started talking about God in a way we'd never heard anybody speak about God. She spoke as though she knew Him! And she knew the Book; she knew the *Tanakh* [Bible] backwards. We didn't know then that she was a Christian. She only talked about the God of Abraham, Isaac and Jacob. She didn't mention Jesus for nine months! She inspired us so much and challenged us to read the Bible for ourselves. This was something we weren't used to because in Judaism, you tend not to do this. After she left on that first night, I picked up the *Torah* [the five books of Moses], which was all we had in the house. Her parting words were, "If you want to know God, just read it." Up until that time I had struggled to read the *Torah*. Maybe it was the language. I just disliked it. Anyway, I decided to read it. In fact we raced each other to read it! We saw the need to read it.

'The more I read of the five books of Moses, the more I realized I'd been misled by the stories I'd been reading in the *Midrash* [a set of commentaries on the *Tanakh*], because they weren't in the *Torah*,' Yoel said.

For Adel, to distance herself from the orthodox community was easy. But for Yoel, then serving in the Rabbinical Corps in the army, this was more difficult. He said: 'Even though I was reading the Bible every day on the bus to and from the base, and we were slowly distancing ourselves from Rabbinical Judaism, I was still appearing to be a Rabbinic Jew during the day. It was only a lot later on, when I'd finished reading the five books of Moses and after I'd read Joshua and Judges, that I began to realize I had a problem with the daily service I had to attend in the synagogue with all the other soldiers. I would go to the synagogue every day with everybody else on the base, but I became aware that they were simply going through the motions of saying the prayers, because they were saying them as fast as they could. Meanwhile, I had started learning these prayers by heart and I couldn't say them that fast and mean what I said. For me that wasn't genuine prayer because if God was there, mumbling away was not relating to God. So I told my fellow soldiers I wouldn't be going to the synagogue with them any more. When they asked me why, I told them they weren't praying, they were just mumbling. I told them I would wait until they'd finished praying, then I would go into the synagogue and pray by myself, and what took them ten minutes would take me half an hour because I would mean every word I spoke. They didn't know what to say, so they accepted that this was important to me, and left me alone.'

'Meanwhile,' Adel continued, 'we maintained a relationship with Judy. She became like family to us.

But Yoel and I were working different shifts; I worked most evenings whereas Yoel worked during the day and had the evening free. So he would spend many hours discussing things to do with the Bible and God with Judy, which meant I was missing out!'

'I began experiencing Scripture,' Yoel added. 'One day as I was reading the book of Joshua, I realized that my bus journey was taking me through the same valley where Joshua chased the Amalekites. I was reading the story in the very place where it happened! I then remembered how the rabbis had told us we are the people of Israel, God's chosen people. But as I read through the Bible I realized we were just a bunch of idiots, and I thought, *Poor God! Why did He choose us? We're stiff-necked.*

'I was embarrassed to associate with so many Jews, who were Zionists and proud. I remember thinking, *Put your head down! We've got nothing to be proud about.* They took such pride in their ancestors. I wanted to tell them to read the Bible, read what really happened and realize that we have a bad track record. Then I noticed all these Gentiles mentioned in the Bible. David's brave men – not many Jews in that list. And who was the good guy in the David and Bathsheba story? Uriah the Hittite.

'Then I started reading Isaiah and for the first time became aware of biblical prophecy. Basic Judaism does not encourage reading the prophets. Today I would say, "Stop the brainwashing!" But the rabbis rule. Until this point the Bible had read like a history book to me. At first I found Isaiah in Hebrew difficult to understand, because it's written in high poetic language. So I started reading it in English and still found it difficult to understand. It felt like a labour of love and I didn't feel I was getting much out of it until I read Isaiah chapter 6.

'This chapter jumped out and slapped me in the face. Because all of a sudden God told Isaiah to go and tell this people, "Be ever hearing, but never understanding; be ever seeing, but never perceiving. Make the heart of this people calloused; make their ears dull and close their eyes. Otherwise they might see with their eyes, hear with their ears, understand with their hearts, and turn and be healed."[1] And all of a sudden, without anybody telling me, I realized the Jewish people are veiled and there's a problem. And I asked myself the question, "Am I veiled? Am I blind? Am I deaf? Is there something that I'm not seeing?"

'I kept reading Isaiah until I reached chapter 53. I didn't understand that chapter; I was blind to its meaning. So I went to see Judy. We didn't know it then, but she'd been praying for nine months for an opportunity to witness to us about Jesus. She'd asked God to give her a sign. So on the day when I knocked on her door and asked her to explain Isaiah 53, she knew this was the sign she'd been praying for. She sat me down with a cup of tea and started telling me about Jesus.

'My initial reaction was to think I'd been deceived. If Judy was a Christian, why hadn't she told me about Jesus before? She kept talking, and as she talked I started to sense what I now know to be the presence of God. I recognized His presence because I had begun to notice it when I was praying in the synagogue on my own. Judy kept on speaking. I fluctuated between feeling deceived and sensing the presence of God. Then gradually the presence of God increased and I knew in my heart that yes, this was it. This was what I'd been looking for all those years.

'Obviously, all the reasons why I shouldn't believe started coming into my mind. Number one, I was a soldier in the Rabbinical Corps; and number two, my Mum would freak out. All my life she had told me, "I will always love you unless you become gay or believe in Jesus." So thoughts of rejection from my family came into my mind. Judy was still speaking. She kept on talking and it sounded like Chinese! Today I know, as an evangelist, that something prevents us from seeing and believing these basic truths. Call it the "veil" if you like.

'Then I said in my mind, *You know what, God? If this is true, then I'm going to go with my heart – I will believe.* And at that moment, as Judy was still witnessing to me, I saw the same vision that I had seen three years before, sitting on my bed in England with the Koran next to me. I saw the face of Jesus. And then I knew, and I told Judy I was ready to believe.

'What happened next seems quite funny today. She gave me a tiny copy of the New Testament and wrapped it in a black plastic bag because in those days, although it was only a few years ago, it was absolutely taboo for us to read the New Testament. She was in secret believer mode. So I took the New Testament home – where I found Adel, sat on our bed, still reading the five books of Moses!

"Something terrible has happened!" I announced. "Jesus is the Messiah!" She looked at me and said, "OK..." and returned to reading her book.'

'I thought that couldn't be true,' Adel admitted. 'I felt disappointed. If there was one thing I was sure about, it was that Christianity was a stupid religion. A guy came along and people followed him and that became a new religion. Was that supposed to be the truth? Call it pride, but I'd been searching so high and so deep, it couldn't possibly be that! I didn't want it to be. At the same time, the fact that Yoel could believe it meant a tremendous change had occurred in his thinking. I knew him so well. Nothing would make him change his mind unless he really believed it. He was such a fanatic! But I wasn't going to believe it just because he believed it. So I withdrew back into myself and decided I needed to check this out for myself.

'I put the *Torah* to one side and read the New Testament that Judy had given Yoel, and was very surprised. I read through Matthew's Gospel and by the end I had tears in my eyes. It was not what I had expected. In the past I'd read some highly philosophical books on religion – pretty heavy stuff. In Matthew's Gospel I couldn't find anything I disagreed with. I was so moved. I became upset and asked myself, *How come I've not read this before?* After all, I'd grown up in Germany where I could easily have read the New Testament, unlike in Israel, where religious Jews are forbidden to read it. I hadn't understood that I was a sinner and needed forgiveness. And so I too came to believe that Jesus was the Messiah. I read Matthew and believed every word.'

Yoel and Adel had to go through a seismic shift in order to believe in Jesus – a process that took them several weeks. Maybe it's difficult for those of us brought up in a Western, Christian culture to fully understand what a huge step it is for a Jewish person to accept that Jesus (so closely linked in their experience to all that is anti-Jewish) is the Messiah. Today, just a few years later, Yoel is a leading team member of Jews for Jesus in Israel, planning to launch the biggest and boldest campaign in the history of the organization, in the country most opposed to hearing such a message. And he and Adel are not yet thirty years old! That this campaign, called 'Behold Your God', is going to make the name of Y'shua an unavoidable issue in Israel is beyond dispute. Nothing like this has happened since the early church burst onto the scene 2,000 years ago. Then the early believers were persecuted and hounded out of Israel. So too were the entire Jewish population in AD 70, and ever since they have moved from country to country, attempting to flee the frequent waves of inquisition and persecution that have swept, restless as the sea, through Europe and Russia, culminating in the Holocaust in the 1940s.

I was interested to find out how Yoel and Adel felt about being involved in such a bold campaign at this time – whether they feared for their safety and what results they were anticipating. After all, if it's successful and many Jewish people living in Israel become Messianic believers, might this change the face of Israeli society as we know it, and even affect the surrounding Arab nations, not to mention the Palestinian people living within Israel as well as in the West Bank and Gaza?

But first we have to hear how they became involved in Jews for Jesus – an organization that is criticized by many in the church for being too direct, and by religious Jews for whom their message is anathema.

Yoel and Adel's story reveals a deep search for God; a search that brought them together in the first place and didn't abate until they found what they were looking for. To enter Judaism and live the religious life with its strict laws obviously caused them considerable disquiet. But undeniably, it has also given them deep insight into the mindset of orthodox Jews living in Israel today. To then join a 'missionary' organization that represents the antithesis of orthodox Judaism is radical! But as Yoel told me, 'I'd heard about Jews for Jesus, that they were the paratroopers of Jewish mission. I was told, "If you join them you'll work till you're dead, then you'll get up and work some more." And I said, "Great! That sounds like the place I belong."'

At first, Yoel was asked to lead the outreach to Shantipi, a New Age festival held in June in northern Israel. Then he was invited to go to New York to get involved with the 'Behold Your God' evangelistic outreach to Jewish people there.

'I loved it,' he told me. 'That week in New York was just a revelation. There was no messing about. We just did it. I liked the professionalism of the organization.' He subsequently visited other cities around the world where similar missions to Jewish people were taking place. And so he entered the training programme to become a full-time 'missionary' with Jews for Jesus, all the time knowing that a campaign for Israel, lasting a number of years, would soon be launched.

'I learnt so much from being involved in the "Behold Your God" campaigns around the world. In Israel, however, it's a completely different animal. What I have felt since becoming an evangelist is a change in the spiritual atmosphere here in Israel. Until recently I felt people were closed; today, it feels as though Israel is more open in a spiritual sense. I feel something is lifting. When it comes to doing "Behold Your God" in Israel now, I am much more scared and less naïve than when I was a new believer. We did a week of testing it out in Tel Aviv in April, and that was the hardest experience of my life. It was like trench warfare. The reality of saturating the media, calling people eight hours a day and standing on the streets, starting in Tel Aviv, is really tough. I am under no illusions and consider martyrdom to be the highest calling there is.

'I also think the next few years of running "Behold Your God" in Israel will be just the beginning. Some people think that after we've brought "Behold Your God" to Jerusalem, Jesus will come back... Maybe they're right – I don't know... I'm wary of being prophetic, but maybe some of the people we're going to lead to the Lord will be part of the 144,000 we read about in the book of Revelation. This certainly could be leading up towards the end!

'And yes, I believe there is going to be an impact on the world because of what's happening here – inevitably. Israel is at the centre of things, whether people like it or not. Part of the reason people get annoyed at Israel – when people are starving in Africa – is because day after day the headline news happens to be about this tiny little country that can't keep its people under control. However, if thousands of Jews voluntarily become believers in Jesus, not as a result of some inquisition, it's going to freak people out and people around the world will start asking questions. A few years ago nobody was doing outreach here, for fear of persecution. But today, the pastors and the students are all talking about it. It's shocking! Recruitment is up. There are going to be lots more evangelists, and as evangelists increase here they will increase elsewhere around the world.'

CHAPTER 2

Ari and Shira Sorko-Ram

The following day was *Shabbat*. I'd arrived late at my beachside hotel in Tel Aviv the night before and was intrigued the next morning to see exactly where I was – overlooking the marina which lies at the northern end of the seafront. The white sandy beach at Tel Aviv is stunning. It stretches for miles. Israelis love to be outside and already I could see people on the beach – some doing keep-fit exercises, others walking or jogging, and many cycling along the promenade.

Later that morning I was due to meet Ari and Shira Sorko-Ram, founders of Maoz Ministries in Israel, at their congregation in downtown Tel Aviv. But first there was time for a stroll. I left the hotel and walked down to the promenade and headed northwards. It was still relatively early but already families were gathering on the beach, children were swimming, teenagers were playing volley-ball. Some were windsurfing. Elderly couples were sitting on the wooden benches placed at regular intervals along the beach-front.

Why am I telling you all this? Because Tel Aviv struck me as being a playground that morning. *Shabbat* may be a 'religious' day for some, but for the majority of Israelis in

32

Tel Aviv it was a day to be outdoors with their family.

And so, I wondered, how many people would be at the Tiferet Y'shua congregation later that morning?

The service, which would be in Hebrew, was due to start at 11 a.m. and I had arranged to meet Shira there. 'Ask the taxi driver to drop you off at the "Cinerama",' she had told me. After what seemed like a long drive, we did eventually arrive outside a Cinerama; it was derelict. The windows were boarded up and a wire security fence encircled the entire building. In one direction the area looked prosperous and well kept, but in the other direction things looked decidedly run down. This was the direction I was heading in. I was on the right road and roughly in the right area, but as I walked up and down, it was impossible to find the right building because there were no numbers visible on the properties. I was about to phone Shira when I saw a group of people go through a doorway. So I followed them. They were the only people around and I hoped they were going to the same place as I was. I followed them up several flights of stairs until I found myself in a large room full of people of all ages. I looked around for Shira, and saw Ari.

The place was alive with conversation. 'There's not so many here today,' said Ari. 'Once a month we have a second service on Friday night. It gives our members a free Saturday so they can do something with their families.' I was amazed. How many more were there?

The service started. They were singing Hebrew worship songs, unfamiliar to me and yet, at the same time, strangely familiar. I felt like an outsider, but also one of them. It was a precious experience.

Tel Aviv may have been a playground for secular Israelis on *Shabbat*, but here I was, with at least 150 enthusiastic Messianic Jewish believers. There was an energy about this congregation, and when Ari stood up to preach, the people listened.

Who are Ari and Shira Sorko-Ram? Ari's mother was a Jewish Russian immigrant to America. Shira's parents were Gordon and Freda Lindsay, founders of Christ for the Nations Bible College in America. Ari became a professional footballer, then a Deputy Sheriff in Los Angeles. Through an interesting series of events, in 1973 he appeared in a Dean Martin movie called *Ricco*, playing a detective. A few years in Hollywood and many films later, Ari, a Messianic Jewish believer, moved permanently to Israel in 1976 in response to Shira's call for Messianic Jews to migrate to Israel.

Shira admits that she spent most of her teens and early twenties away from the faith. 'My parents' persevering prayers brought me back to God,' she told me. After living for three years in Israel, she decided to move there permanently and likens herself to Ruth, the Moabite, who said, 'Your God shall be my God, and your people shall be my people.' Ari and Shira met in 1976. They married in 1977 and that same year started their first congregation in Herzeliya (a northern suburb of Tel Aviv). In those days, as will emerge from other stories in this book, the numbers of Messianic Jewish believers in Israel were extremely small.

To hear more of their story and their 'take' on *Israel's New Disciples*, after lunch I went with them to the Maoz offices in a downtown building near their congregation in Tel Aviv.

Ari wasted no time. 'One of the most important things we feel we are involved with at present is getting Israel back into her rightful position. Not a better position or a lesser position; Israel is no better than any other nation. It's like a family – the husband isn't better than the wife, but there has to be a biblical order so that the purposes of God can move in the family. The Body of Messiah is also a family; there is one Father, one Messiah and one Holy Spirit.

'So when Paul says, "I am not ashamed of the gospel, because it is the power of God for the salvation of everyone who believes: first for the Jew, then for the Gentile",[1] that's God's rule for evangelism. It's always been that way and has never changed. People have said, some aggressively, others passively, "Well, Israel will come in eventually," based on one scripture in Zechariah where it says, "They will look on me, the one they have pierced, and they will mourn for him as one mourns for an only child, and grieve bitterly for him as one grieves for a firstborn son."[2] But you can't base a theology on one verse! God has always intended that Israel be an integral part of His plan to reach the nations. His idea was that Jew and Gentile would go together and reach the nations. So for the purposes of God, it's really critical, we believe, that Israel gets back into its rightful position, as we read in Romans 11: "Did they stumble so as to fall beyond recovery? Not at all! Rather, because of their transgression, salvation has come to the Gentiles to make Israel envious."[3] Why?

'So that the Jews would get back into their right biblical position and Jew and Gentile would work together. Paul reveals to us that when Israel is brought back into a personal relationship with her God, it will be followed by a great spiritual awakening among the nations of the world. As Paul wrote, "If their [the Jews'] fall is riches for the world, and their failure riches for the Gentiles, how much more their fullness?... For if their being cast away is the reconciling of the world, what will their acceptance be but life from the dead [for the Gentiles]?"[4]

'In other words,' Ari went on, 'Israel's reconciliation with the God of Israel through Y'shua, the King of the Jews, will bring great spiritual benefits to all the world. There are so many verses in the Old Testament that confirm this, such as are found in the prophets Isaiah and Zechariah:

Now it shall come to pass in the latter days
That the mountain of the Lord's house
Shall be established on the top of the mountains...
And all nations shall flow to it.
Many people shall come and say,
'Come, and let us go up to the mountain of the Lord,
To the house of the God of Jacob...'
For out of Zion shall go forth the law,
And the word of the Lord from Jerusalem.[5]

Yes, many peoples and strong nations
Shall come to seek the Lord of hosts in Jerusalem,
And to pray before the Lord.[6]

'I am coming and I will dwell in your
[Israel's] midst,' says the Lord. 'Many
nations shall be joined to the Lord in that
day, and they shall become My people.'[7]

'In whatever order these events take place is not our concern. We simply want to understand God's plan as given us in the Scriptures and be a part of it in our generation.'

I was interested to ask Ari and Shira what evidence

they were seeing of Israel getting back into their rightful biblical position (after almost 2,000 years of being out of it).

Ari continued, 'I think things have begun. The fact that a number of Israelis, especially in the establishment, are aware there is a Messianic Jewish community here today who believe in a Jewish Messiah called Y'shua, and remain Jewish, is significant. In the past, Jews who came to believe in Y'shua were no longer perceived as Jewish because it was considered they had converted to Christianity and therefore sacrificed their Jewish identity.

'Many years ago we had a government investigation into our congregation when one of our members was taken to court by her husband who accused her of leaving the Jewish faith, and he wanted custody of their children. Government social workers duly visited our congregation and as a result of their investigation concluded that we were a Messianic Jewish congregation and had not left the faith of Abraham and Moses and that we were still Jewish. Even though they did not agree with us as to who the Messiah was, they recognized that our expression was a Jewish expression of what we believed. So the spiritual climate is changing.

'When we used to say to people that Y'shua is the Messiah, they would ask us if we were talking about Joshua [Jehoshua]. It was such a strange concept to them. "What are you talking about?" they would say. When they understood who we were talking about they would reply, "Do you believe in Yeshu as the Messiah?" And we would say, "No, *Y'shua* is His name." In Israel, non-believers call Jesus "Yeshu". Actually, it is the initials for a curse. We always correct them and tell them his name is Y'shua.

'When you use the Hebrew word for Jesus – Y'shua – they understand the name comes from the root meaning "salvation, *the* Messiah, the anointed one". Even when they hear the word "Jesus" in English, it means something different to them – like Jesus is His first name and Christ is His last. They don't know the significance of His name in English. Gradually they begin to understand you're talking about covenant relationship, the King of Israel, the sacrifice, the son of David – Mashiach Ben David. And they realize, because we are Jewish, that we're not coming from a Christian perspective (which Jewish people are very suspicious of). And so there's a process of re-education taking place in Israel that's beginning to catch on. And there's an openness in the Israeli community, including the academic community, to reinvestigate the question of whether or not Y'shua is the Messiah.

'For a long time pressure was exerted through the influence of the orthodox community, who say "No, you can't look." It caused such feelings of guilt and distrust that the majority of Jewish people have never considered these things nor dared to read the New Testament. But today, people are openly looking into the Scriptures and examining who Y'shua is. He is being talked about on the radio and television. Books and articles are being written about Him. So there is an earnest interest to find out exactly where He fits in. There is a spiritual awakening in Israeli society.

'In the past forty years, things have moved forward a long way and I think we're at the beginning of revival. We're not in revival, but we see a change of heart. We see the openness. We see people coming off the street into a congregational meeting, not knowing what they're coming to, and they leave born again with a new heart and a new spirit! When they come into a congregation and see Israelis singing songs to God in Hebrew and reading the

Scriptures in Hebrew, they say, "This is for us." And it is a numbers thing here in Israel. In the Jewish community, if you only have a group of, let's say ten believers, people don't pay much attention to the beliefs of ten people. But think of the larger impact you have when you are a hundred believers. They begin to say, "That number of people can't totally be off their rocker!"'

So if Ari and Shira have seen the Israeli public become more curious about Y'shua in recent years, I asked them to look forward five to ten years and describe what they are expecting to happen next in Israel.

Ari began, 'I see a significant growth in the numbers of Messianic Jewish believers. Right now we have between 10,000 and 15,000 believers living in Israel. Of those, approximately 2,000 are *Sabras*, meaning they were born here. I think there's going to be a significant increase over the next five years, with more congregations owning their own property and meeting in larger buildings, which in turn will attract more attention and interest from local Israelis.

'I also think there is going to be an awakening in the church at large [i.e. the Gentile church in the nations] to realize that Israel is the *first fruits*. The Lord is the Lord of the harvest. What the church does with Israel will impact what God does over the whole world. We are praying that the church, as we read in Romans 11, will come not just to provoke Israel but rather to provoke Israel to jealousy, and support the body of believers here, just as the orthodox community around the world supports the orthodox Jewish community here in Israel. If the Christian community around the world started to support the Messianic Jewish community here in a greater measure, five years from now, I don't think we'll recognize the Body of Messiah.

'I also anticipate we're going to see the young generation impacted, especially on the university campuses. Israeli young people today are searching for something real; their search is taking them all over the world. We believe that if the message of Y'shua gets to this young generation they'll take a hold of it and run with it. After finishing the army, Israeli youth rush to visit places like India. I remember reading in the paper that one Indian guru there said that Israelis are the most "spiritual" of all the young travellers coming to India.'

Shira added, 'It's helpful when talking about future trends to mention what has happened in the last forty years. In 1967, when I arrived here in Israel, there were just a handful of believers. I only remember meeting one adult *Sabra* at that time and he had a lot of mental problems – his mother had come out of the Holocaust. There were quite a few Christian missionaries in 1967 but the gap between them and the Jewish people was huge. They weren't connecting because Jewish people thought that Christian missionaries were trying to finish what the Holocaust had tried to do – destroy the Jewish people. How? By spiritually destroying them, encouraging them to leave their Jewish traditions and convert to Christianity. And they saw that as a spiritual holocaust. They looked upon missionaries with fear. "We are afraid they are going to wipe the Jews out by getting us to convert to Christianity and abandon our Jewish identity," I was once told by a Jewish person. So when I first arrived in Israel in 1967, that was the atmosphere.

'The term "Messianic Jew" began to emerge around the time of the Yom Kippur war in 1973; until then people had never heard such a name. However, over these past forty years things have changed considerably.

'I'll give you an example. I'm trying to lose some weight, so I have a trainer who I meet once a week. At first I didn't tell him anything about my faith. Then he asked me what I did, so I told him about the Messianic Jews. The moment I mentioned that he said, "Oh, I have a friend who is a Messianic Jew." So for him I wasn't a problem. Many people have a relative who has become a Messianic Jew. And so we are seeing that as the numbers of believers increase, the walls of fear and suspicion are being broken down.

'Then in the early 1990s the Russians started pouring into Israel, forcing the country to become more liberal. Of the 1 million Russians who have immigrated to Israel, it is estimated that at least 200,000 to 300,000 of them are not rabbinically Jewish because they do not have the paperwork to prove their Jewish background. So the Israeli government had to relax the law of return to accommodate these people, and in so doing, it loosened up the thinking of the Jewish people. Unfortunately, with liberality comes acceptance of a lot of things. For example, in the 1960s there was no openly gay movement of any kind in this country. Thieving was unheard of – you could leave your door unlocked and not worry. We never heard of anybody being murdered. So in many ways Israel has gone downhill. But, at the same time, we have seen God use the window of opportunity that has been created by this rise in liberal behaviour, because with it has come a greater interest in and tolerance towards Messianic Jews by many in Israeli society.

'There is another aspect of Israel's history that Ari and I find very interesting. Between the time of the resurrection of Jesus and the destruction of the Temple in AD 70 there was a forty-year period. Up until this time God had largely confined Himself to dealing with the Jewish people, although it is clear from the Scriptures that He also cared about the other nations of the world and had a plan for their salvation too. The period between AD 30 and AD 70 was the time when the early church began, and at first the believers were mainly Jewish. There were many Jews saved in this period. We read in Acts how 3,000 were saved in one day and 5,000 on another day. Gentiles were being saved as well as Jewish people, so it was not an exclusively Jewish movement, rather a mixture of Jew and Gentile. However, after AD 70, when the Jewish believers were forced out of Jerusalem along with the rest of the Jewish population, and had to take refuge in the surrounding nations, their testimony resulted in many Gentiles becoming believers and joining their own assemblies, and so the time of the Gentiles began. Gradually the number of Gentile believers increased until they greatly outnumbered the Jewish believers, and as we now realize, the church took on a non-Jewish identity – until today.

'Whilst we don't prophesy about dates, it's interesting that in 1967, after the Six Day War, Jerusalem came back into the hands of the Jewish people. This suggests to us that the time of the Gentiles is ending, and for the past forty years we have been moving towards a time when God is again bringing his salvation to the Jews. This does not mean that in 2007 the time of the Gentiles was up! But what we have seen is that more and more Jews have been receiving the Lord, just as more and more Gentiles began to receive salvation between AD 30 and AD 70. At the same time, since 1967 there have also been great revivals amongst Gentiles all over the world.'

I was intrigued to hear Shira talking like this. Could it be that Ari and Shira are correct in their analysis of recent historical facts and their understanding of how God is now reconnecting Jewish and Gentile believers?

Ari chipped in, 'Can I add something to support that? During that forty-year period from the resurrection of Messiah in AD 30 to the destruction of the Temple in AD 70, there was a process of revelation going on in the hearts and minds of the disciples of Y'shua and the Apostles that made them realize that the Gentiles could be born again as Gentiles [i.e. not having to become Jews] – and that salvation came to the Jews not just for the Jews' sake but for the sake of all the nations in the world. And that revelation was a big one. The Apostle Paul's letter to the Galatians details this – how Gentiles do not need to be circumcised to come into the New Covenant, for example. It was a process that took a long time to catch on. And now today we're seeing the same thing happening again. Since 1967, when the Messianic Jewish movement began to burst into life, some in the Gentile community began to understand that whilst they had had the message for 2,000 years, now it was time to go back and give the message to the Jewish people in Israel. Through their understanding of Scripture, it dawned on them that the Messiah is coming back to a people who say, "Blessed is he who comes in the name of the Lord." They realized He's not coming back to Moscow or New York; rather, He's coming back to a Jewish nation that is waiting for Him. Today we observe that many in the nations are waking up. We see that something is happening all over the world and many in the Christian community are saying, "Wait a minute, what about Israel?" And I think those who understand the heart of God are saying, "Let's get Israel back where Israel belongs so that the purposes of God can be fulfilled with Jew and Gentile together."'

Ari and Shira were speaking with such intensity now. Any post-lunch stupor had evaporated and now they were sitting upright with their elbows on the table, looking intently at me as if to say, *Do you understand what we're saying?* We had got to the heart of what motivates them. Sitting there at the boardroom table in the Maoz offices, I realized just how many hours they must have spent discussing and praying about the times in which we are now living, in their desire to understand what the Bible has to say about these things. And it was obvious that they saw their destiny as inextricably linked to Israel's destiny. What was also emerging was that with that realization came a great responsibility. What was their role? What should they do next?

Shira continued, 'To confirm what Ari was saying, before AD 30, during the time of the Jews, basically you had to be a Jew to be in God's covenant, and if a Gentile wanted to become a part of God's people, they had to become Jewish. Ruth is a good example of this. Similarly, during the time of the Gentiles, from AD 70 until 1967, if a Jew wanted to get saved, with few exceptions, he became a Gentile. If he accepted Jesus Christ he lost his Jewish identity and became a Gentile, with the result that the Jewish believers disappeared into Christianity. However, since 1967, exactly the opposite has happened. When a Jew becomes a believer today, he realizes he can remain a Jew!

'I don't know when the Lord's coming back; it seems to me it's getting closer and closer. I believe the Lord is waiting, just as the farmer waits for the harvest, for the Jews to be saved, and parallel to that, for a great spiritual awakening among the nations.'

'So what needs to happen?' I asked. 'What

responsibility do you think the Gentile church has towards the Messianic believers here in Israel today?'

'I think Paul makes it clear,' Shira said. 'He says in Romans 11, that if people want to see their own nation come into revival, they have to put Israel first. "To the Jew first" – that's what the Bible says. If the church will first help Israel, then God has promised He will spread the gospel throughout the world. What else could these verses in Romans 11 mean? Can we look at them once more? "Now if [Israel's] fall is [spiritual] riches for the world... how much more [Israel's] fullness?" And as if Paul wants to make sure we get the message, he repeats himself three verses down: "For if their being cast away is the reconciling of the world, what will their acceptance be but life from the dead [for the world]?"

'And when we visit churches in other countries, that's what we tell them. We say, "Look, God has promised that if you will bless Israel and help Israel have revival, then in turn He will bless you. 'I will bless those who bless you.'"[8] Many Christians understand this in part and they give to hospitals and other wonderful projects in this country. But we need help to evangelize the Jewish people! Israel will remain a dark nation that is full of war and trouble; we will not have peace or revival until the church gets in here and helps us.'

Shira's voice was trembling as she spoke. Ari was sitting quietly looking at his wife. I was looking at two people who clearly felt frustrated and at times alone and isolated, feeling that the church is not supporting them in the way it should. They know their destiny. And they know Israel's destiny. But for them something is missing.

'Yes,' Ari took up the conversation, 'just to affirm that, most Gentiles really can't come here and evangelize unless they speak Hebrew. God is not a political Zionist – there is no political solution. There is no government that can solve the problems here. There is no treaty that will work; the only thing that can bring about change is the salvation of the Jewish people – or as Paul calls it, "life from the dead". And Christians need that revelation. Giving to secular Israel is biblical. But it's more biblical to give to the priesthood. Even if 10 per cent of the money that is given by the Christian church to Israel was given to the believers here, it would revolutionize our ability to reach our people!

'Also, it's not the role of the Christian community to take political decisions for Israel and to press the Israeli government – that's Israel's role. It's the role of the church to pray for God's will and purposes for Israel. Israel's destiny is to be a "light to the nations".[9] Israel has no other purpose for existing. Being a light to the nations started in the Abrahamic covenant: "all families of the earth will be blessed through you". [10] That blessing is the salvation of the nations – a spiritual light. God has brought Israel back in a physical sense... but now the spiritual side of Israel has to wake up, just as we read in Ezekiel,when God told the prophet to prophesy to the dry bones. It says in the Scriptures that "In those days ten men from all languages and nations will take firm hold of one Jew by the hem of his robe and say, 'Let us go with you, because we have heard that God is with you.'"[11] Israel's destiny is to reveal the salvation of God to the nations. And yes, there's an awakening today in this nation – but not the revival the Bible is talking about.

'We know something's going on because the opposition we're getting is intense. It works on three different fronts. Messianic believers are frequently harassed by the Jewish orthodox community; they can get very aggressive and often indulge in physical protest and intimidation.

'Secondly, the government tries hard to prohibit Messianic Jewish believers from coming to live in Israel; whilst for those already living here, if they are known as believers, getting a job can be difficult. This means some of our people find it hard to manage financially.

'And then we have pressure from within. In order to feed his family the average congregational leader has to work full time as well as pastor his congregation. I don't know of a congregation in the country that can totally support itself. Few congregations own their own building. I know of one congregation that met for a year in the forest before they finally found a place to meet.

'I think the devil is aware that when Israel comes to faith, it means that Messiah is coming back. If all the nations come to faith but not Israel, Messiah's not coming back. But when Israel comes to faith the purposes of God will go forward. There will be great revival. Israel will be involved throughout the nations and we're going to see a huge move of the Spirit.

'I think this is the most significant time in history. Ezekiel speaks to us:

> For I will take you out of the nations; I will
> gather you from all the countries and bring
> you back into your own land. I will sprinkle
> clean water on you, and you will be clean;
> I will cleanse you from all your impurities
> and from all your idols. I will give you a
> new heart and put a new spirit in you; I will
> remove from you your heart of stone and

> give you a heart of flesh. And I will put my
> Spirit in you and move you to follow my
> decrees and be careful to keep my laws.[12]

So, if Israel's destiny is to be a light to the nations, that suggests that Israel will increasingly be getting involved and sharing her "light" with the nations.'

Ari then told me a true story concerning the poorest country in the world, with the highest illiteracy rate in the world – Burkina Faso.

'They are so poor, the lifespan is only 49 years and 20 per cent of the children die before the age of 5. One day, out of the blue, we received a letter from a pastor from Burkina Faso called Ram Zango. Ram went to Christ for the Nations Bible College in Dallas. His father was a witchdoctor but Ram became a Christian when he went to university to study engineering. Then, after he'd been to Bible College, he went back to his country as a minister.

'He saw the poverty and desperate need amongst his people and he told them, "We must bless Israel" – he had learnt the biblical principles of believing quite literally what the Bible said. Ram found one local pastor called Jean who really grasped this principle, but he didn't have any money. However, like every other person in Burkina Faso, they grew their own crops to feed their families. So they decided to partition off a corner of his field, and the crops they grew there they sold in the market to raise money to send to Israel.

'Eventually the church saved $7 and gave the money to Ram Zango to send to Israel. But Ram found out that to send the money, the exchange rate and stamps would be more than the $7. And so, in order to honour Jean's faith in raising this money, he took a loan from the bank and sent the money to Israel. Then God began to bless this little community. They dug a well and found water only a few metres down, which meant they could water their crops, and so the yield from their land gradually increased. News about this spread to neighbouring villages as Ram began telling them about how God had blessed this community since they had started blessing Israel. A phenomenon started taking place. The villages where there were churches sending money to Israel received much more rain than the surrounding villages.

'Three years after Ram Zango had sent the first gift of $7, we here at Maoz received two letters from Burkina Faso with $2,000 in cash enclosed in each. Our accountant started crying as he read the letters from Ram Zango. Each time they sent more. God was prospering their crops.

'We said, "We're meant to be a light to the nations. They are blessing Israel – how can we help them?" So we went out there!

'We had no idea what to expect. We travelled from village to village, and it was so hot – over 100 degrees! Almost no paved roads! But we did it and photographed what we saw. Once we'd seen the situation for ourselves, we started discussing what we could do to help these people. Shira met an Israeli businessman...'

Shira explained: 'I showed him pictures I had taken of these poverty-stricken Christians in Burkina Faso blessing Israel by sending money to us. He said, "Have you noticed that the poorest countries in Africa are the ones which are French speaking? When the British were in Africa, whilst they weren't perfect, they built roads and electricity and provided infrastructure. But the French just raped the countries they were involved in – countries like Niger, Chad, Benin and Burkina Faso, so that today they're economically at the bottom of the nations." That sank into our hearts and we decided we didn't want to be like the French, who just took from these people...'

Ari continued: 'And so we looked at ways in which Israel could help Burkina Faso. After all, we have some of the leading experts in irrigation and agriculture for desert and sub-desert regions. The people in Burkina Faso need food. They have about four months when enough rain falls, enabling them to grow their crops. But then they sit waiting for the next rains, hoping they will have enough food to last until then – and if the rains don't come, there is disaster. There is water in Burkina Faso because a number of Western countries have built dams for the Burkinabe people, but because they don't have the technology to take the water out of the lakes to irrigate their land, only a couple of government farms can make use of the dams, and even they have very low technological know-how. The people at large are unable to grow food during the dry season.

'A little while after our first trip, we were invited back to Burkina Faso to speak to some of their government officials. They were keen to hear how Israel might help their country, and in exchange they offered to give us many hundreds of acres of land to irrigate! We said we didn't want hundreds of acres. We told them we didn't want to bring sacks of food; rather, we wanted to build an Agriculture Training Centre to teach the people to grow their own food. "We don't want to profit," we told them, "we want your people to profit." And they were pleased to cooperate with us.'

Shira continued: 'When we started to look at ways

of helping those people, we realized the majority were agriculturists – 90 per cent of the Burkinabe people exist through farming. We realized that if we could raise their level of agricultural knowledge even a little bit, it would raise the economic level of the whole country. And so we contacted a programme here in Israel, that Golda Meir actually started, called MASHAV, which brings Africans and some Asians for special courses to introduce them to new concepts of farming. They agreed that if we paid the air fares, they would take a number of people from Burkina Faso into their courses.

'So we did that, and the MASHAV people, in a *kibbutz* not far from here, got really excited, because Ram Zango was one of the people we brought over, and Ram is electric! He has a personality that demands love and respect; he's so enthusiastic and happy. Everybody loves him instantly. And so, from a $7 gift, they now have the world's best experts helping them.

'We believe the nation of Burkina Faso will be transformed by the training farms we are wanting to set up. This knowledge will surely spill over to the French-speaking countries around Burkina Faso as they see the Burkinabe Christians prospering with new farming techniques. And they will know from Ram that it all started because they blessed Israel.'

CHAPTER 3

David and Lisa Loden

The next day was Sunday; time to leave Tel Aviv and head north, along the coast, to Netanya. A few years ago Netanya was a small town; but with the recent influx of thousands of Russian Jewish immigrants, it has grown into a large, thriving city.

I was on my way to meet David and Lisa Loden. They suggested the quickest way to travel was by train. Having never boarded a train in Israel before, I thought this was a great idea. The whole experience was an interesting one from the start. Buying a ticket at Tel Aviv was frenetic. There were crowds of soldiers milling around. Many of them were travelling south to Beer Sheva, whilst others were going my way. The platforms in both directions were crammed with people, so when the train arrived, I was swept into an already full carriage, and needless to say, it was standing room only!

I glanced around at the other passengers. Standing next to me was a teenage Muslim girl. Perhaps she was a student. Directly in front of us were an ultra-orthodox Jewish couple; he was engrossed in his prayer book, whilst his wife looked passively out of the window. Lost in their own thoughts and seemingly oblivious to the sea of humanity pressing around them, neither altered their gaze. People from different worlds cheek by jowl on a crowded train. Apart from the Muslim girl, the orthodox Jewish couple and me, as far as I could see, all the other passengers were Israeli soldiers – as many women as men, all dressed in the same brown uniform of trousers and shirt. Rifles were slung over shoulders. Bags were everywhere. Some were so tired that they sank to the floor and leant against whoever or whatever they were next to and fell asleep.

As I looked at the people around me in that crowded railway carriage, it was as though I was looking at a cross-section of Israeli society – a society where there are distinct identities. They were all dressed in 'uniform': the Muslim girl, the orthodox couple, the soldiers. They had no need to speak to identify themselves; their appearance said it all.

This matter of identity was to feature in the conversation I was about to have with David and Lisa Loden. Originally hippies in America, they came to live in Israel thirty-three years ago. From nothing, they started a local congregation that today is thriving. As pastors they have a particular passion for young people and also for Arab/Palestinian people. Their story is similar to those of many other Messianic Jewish leaders; it is quite uncanny how many of them were hippies in America in the 1960s.

David met me at Netanya's railway station, and as we drove through the leafy suburbs to their home, along streets lined with orange and lemon trees and bougainvillea spilling over garden walls, he told me how busy he and Lisa were. The congregation was growing, many Russian immigrants had moved into Netanya and there were many social problems. It was some years since I'd seen

David, and as I listened to him, it seemed as though the years spent pioneering in Israel, far from wearying him, had sharpened him. And here he was, over thirty years on, looking back on so much change in Israeli society and growth in the congregation, and at the same time looking forward, believing that the best was yet to come.

It was good to visit their home again, a house they had built in the early 1980s. I was struck by the huge mango tree that shaded much of their front garden. They had put up nets to catch the fruit. There had been so much, they had enjoyed fresh mangoes for weeks!

David and Lisa live next door to Evan and Maala Thomas. Together they share the work of leading the congregation in Netanya. I saw Evan in the garden – he was busy watering the plants and tidying things up. I would be back the next day to speak with him.

Meanwhile, whilst David made some coffee, I spoke with Lisa.

'God is definitely active and on the move,' she said. 'And this is more evident today than it's ever been in our time here. We're seeing a surge of young people in the twenty-plus age group coming to faith in Messiah in this country and forming a grass-roots movement that's fuelled with a tremendous amount of energy.

'We live in a postmodern world and Israel is a place of tension and conflict. It's just there, and consequently it's part of the consciousness of the people here. You don't necessarily feel the danger and the tension every single day, but it's part of your life.

'Added to that, the young people growing up here are living in a spiritual vacuum. Judaism has disappointed them. The political ideology of Israel enjoyed by their parents and grandparents has not come through to this generation. We've been living through a time of tremendous questioning, doubt and uncertainty, and all the time there exists a continual threat of war. Living like this forces people to look for meaning, and so there is a spiritual search going on in this country – a longing not just for stability, but a longing too to understand why we are here.

'People ask, what's this all about? Why can't we just be like the other nations? And of course Israel cannot be like any other nation. We know that as a nation and a people we are different. And we are judged. The world judges Israel not according to the standards by which they judge every other nation – whatever we do is criticized. This atmosphere creates a sense of narrowness, confinement and instability in our young people, so it's not surprising that we have a lot of social problems in this country.

'This generation is searching for meaning. Whilst we are seeing many young people coming to faith and bringing a new energy and a new excitement into our congregations, other young people go looking for meaning in the East. For example, there are thousands of young Israelis who go to India. The postmodern attitude says everyone should find their own truth.

'It's a complex picture and it's gradually changing the face of Israeli society because young people, in general, are more open and bolder than their parents' generation. They are willing to consider anything and they will read the forbidden books and they will be attracted to something that doesn't fit the normal mould, because the normal mould no longer satisfies anyway.

'The implications of having so many young people who are prepared to challenge the status quo are far reaching. We sense that an underground movement has begun that is ready to emerge very powerfully and affect the thinking of the youth in Israel. As more and more come to faith in Messiah, this has the potential to affect the whole of Israeli life and society. If I look forward five, even ten years, I see, alongside the traditional congregational structure, a growing number of smaller groups of believers with a greater focus on community living. This means they will become more visible within Israeli society. In addition, there is something happening, in the believing community, in the area of music and youth culture that will impact society at large.'

I was interested to hear from Lisa what these young Messianic Jewish believers, the majority of whom have been born in Israel (unlike many of their parents, who were immigrants), think when they start to understand the Scriptures. What is their understanding of the biblical role of the Jewish people and the nation of Israel both now and in the future?

'Whilst they embrace the notion that Israel and the Jewish people are different in the eyes of God to all the other nations, at the same time they understand the bigger picture of God's heart for the world. Modern secular Israel is influenced by humanistic liberal thought which tends to be alternative and leaning to the left. I have noticed that every Jewish believer, at some point in his life, experiences an identity crisis. The factors that make up our identity as Messianic believers are very complex, and people have to find different answers and different ways of living out their understanding of who they are, both in relation to modern Israeli society and also in relation to the Scriptures. Whilst we understand from the Scriptures that Israel is special in God's eyes, so too we understand that God has a heart for the entire world. For the young

Israeli, when they come to faith, they have to be taught what that really means and how to live that out.

'As pastors, David and I help them by encouraging them to study the Word of God. We believe this is very important, because otherwise they could be carried away by enthusiasm, and they need to be rooted and grounded in their faith, settled and established, living their lives uprightly, ethically, morally and at the same time having a real heart for people. And what we see in them is a tremendous heart and passion for people, because our nation without God is lost; we're very aware of that. So yes, they are a generation of passionate evangelists. They believe that the fight is on for the soul of this nation because the forces of darkness are powerful here, both within society and also the threat from without. And there's something about living in a country where you have a constant threat from without; a threat against your very survival. That does something to you – it shapes you and forms you at a very basic level. Our young people have grown up with that threat and many want to break out from that, rebel against it, move away, spend five years in India... But then when they meet the Lord, they find they have become part of another society and culture that penetrates the context of where they live.'

Are they starting to understand their role in relation to Israel being 'a light to the nations'?[1] Do they talk about that at all?

'Yes, they do. First, at a local level, they see the need to be seen standing together and being "the one new man in Messiah".[2] At the same time, they humbly understand Israel's destiny before God. All the young believers I know have a strong sense that their lives must show forth the life of Messiah, and they're very open and bold in their conversations with their friends, their fellow students and their workmates – they don't hide their faith at all.'

Lisa had given an up-to-the-minute assessment of developments in the Messianic Jewish community. Now I was keen to put the clock back thirty-three years and hear how their story had unfolded and whether the vision she and David had when they first came to Israel had yet been realized. After all, they had left America on a one-way ticket and arrived in Israel knowing only that it was right to come, but not knowing how things were going to work out. By 1982 they had established themselves in Netanya and by 1989 had designed and built the house where we were sitting that morning. So what had been their vision in those early days?

'We had a twofold vision. My husband, because he's a musician, wanted to produce a hymnology in Hebrew for the then barely visible Messianic community – to write the new songs for the new generation. And the second part of our vision at that time was to see, springing up in this country, warm homes, places of refuge – not physical refuge but spiritual refuge, again for the barely visible community. We understood from our reading of the Scriptures that God wanted to move in this country and that He would bring the Israeli people to faith in our day.

'When we arrived there were no more than 500 believers in the entire land. It was hard work and it felt very different to the life we'd been living in America. We knew people had laboured in this country for their entire lives and never seen a person come to faith. And we knew that their prayers and their tears had watered and softened the ground, and we were the generation that would see that bear fruit even if it took ten, twenty or thirty years. Because God gives you joy in whatever

He calls you to do, whilst it was tough, it wasn't a heavy burden, because this nation has a promise that no other nation has – we know we're labouring in the field that will bear fruit. The book of Romans speaks quite clearly on this issue when Paul says, "My heart's desire and prayer to God for the Israelites is that they may be saved."[3] And he adds, "… what will their acceptance be but life from the dead?"[4] From that we understand that the return of the Jewish people to God has been His intention from the beginning and He will accomplish it.'

David and Lisa Loden have always had a heart for the Arab people too. They have both been involved with Musalaha (the organization founded by Salim Munayer to encourage reconciliation between Jewish believers and Arab Christians). Until it became impossible for Jewish people to enter Bethlehem, David taught at the Bethlehem Bible College. So where did that heart for the Arab people come from?

'The experiences of our early years in faith are probably foundational for all of us. When we came to faith we were the different ones [i.e. hippies]; yet we were embraced by our local church, which was a multi-generational, multicultural congregation and included a large number of Native Americans. So we understood from the beginning that God's heart is inclusive – that race, gender and generations do not matter in the eyes of God; rather, His desire is for His people to be one. So when we came to Israel we quickly realized that Israel is not just a country of Jews, but is also a country with a very large Arab population. In this Arab population are Arab believers in Jesus – Arab Christians – and we understood from our 'spiritual DNA' that these were our brothers and sisters, and we must be in relationship with one another.

'One of the first things I got involved with in the seventies was a women's prayer meeting in the north – a monthly meeting that continues to this day. It was dynamic. Two or three women came from Netanya, four or five from Haifa, and we'd meet in Tiberias or in an Arab village. It was a very simple meeting; one of the women might give a very short talk, then we would share our prayer needs and pray for each other. What united us then, and unites us to this day, is concern for our people to come to faith in Messiah – both Jews and Arabs. Whilst you may say our peoples and our cultures are so different, we found we had much in common. Mothers have children. And these children were growing up in a hostile society; a hostile Jewish society and a hostile Arab society. Meeting together to pray, we found a place where our hearts touched, and we sensed our common needs for our families and our children. From there it was only natural to reach beyond the family into our society.'

I asked Lisa whether they experienced much resistance from Messianic believers who couldn't understand their reasons and motivations for meeting with Palestinian people, especially as the troubles increased and the security tightened.

'In the early years, no. Before we had *intifadas*, things were quiet. But more recently, particularly since we've been involved not only with the Arab Israeli Christians but also the Arab Christians who live in the Palestinian Administered Territories, there have been a lot of questions. "How can you have fellowship with people who don't believe what we believe about Israel?" We had to focus on the primary issues and not allow the secondary issues, no matter how important they are, to hinder our expression of unity. I don't underestimate

60

the importance of the secondary issues, but we could not allow them to come between us. We focused on being reconciled to each other through the blood of Jesus that was shed for all of us. Matters of nationalism, biblical Zionism and the place of Israel were subjects we would work through together at the appropriate time. First we had to build bridges of trust, and we did this by listening to each other's stories; hearing and understanding where the other person was coming from. To this day we find it can take a long time before we approach the Scriptures together; you come with an open mind and an open heart. You listen; you care for people. And however important the secondary issues are, we concentrate on our identity as believers in Messiah.

'Having said that, we have found that for some people the matter of nationalism is very important because it's part of their self-identity. Recently we had a women's conference in Cyprus where we brought together five small groups of women. Some of these groups had met for four years, whilst others had only started in the past year. We decided we were going to deal with the issue of identity. What is our identity? For a long time we talked about our identity in Messiah and we all agreed without question that this was our primary identity. Then we did an exercise where we put chairs in the middle of the room and the chairs were labelled. Every woman chose the "spiritual chair" as her primary identity; her primary identity was in Messiah. Then we asked the Arab group to identify how they described themselves: were they Arab Israeli, Palestinian or Arab Christian? Similarly, with the Jewish women, we asked them how they would describe themselves: a Hebrew Christian, a Christian, a Messianic Jew or simply a Jew?

This was a very interesting exercise because we saw the validity and importance of these other aspects of our identity, and we were then able to recognize each other's self-identity, whether Jewish or Arab. We then took this a step further and gave each woman the opportunity to say why she had chosen that particular chair. This produced some surprises! On the Israeli side, one native-born *Sabra* Israeli woman identified herself only as Christian. Why? Because her faith was her most important form of identity. She didn't identify herself as Messianic. She didn't identify herself as Israeli. Only Christian. That was the only chair in which she felt comfortable.'

I was surprised to hear this story because the word 'Christian' in a Jewish context has been anathema for centuries.

'Exactly!' Lisa agreed. 'Then,' she quickly continued, 'on the Arab side some of the sisters who lived in Nazareth chose to be identified as Palestinian rather than as Israeli Arabs. It was a wonderful exercise because they were able to talk about why they chose that chair.

'Then there was a chair marked "Foreigner" for women who were married to an Arab or a Jew even though they themselves were from another nation. We were surprised to see one of the Jewish immigrants choose this chair, because she had never felt comfortable as an Israeli. And so we learnt how important it is to give one another space; we are all on a journey. Where I am today I will not be next month. Most have moved on. But some have moved out because they found it too challenging.

'There are some wonderful stories emerging as a result of these encounters. I know of a Palestinian Christian woman who lives in the Ramallah area, and a Jewish sister who lives in an Israeli settlement. The Jewish sister came to the checkpoint to pick up the Palestinian woman and the Palestinian woman went to spend the night with her in her settlement. It was made possible because of a brief window of opportunity over a holiday period when sometimes permission is given for people to leave a Palestinian area for a short while. The Jewish sister is a *Sabra* [born in Israel]. She grew up here – she is Israeli through and through! When she became a believer she became very focused on Messianic Jewish identity. So to move from that point to picking up a Palestinian sister at the checkpoint was a huge journey!

'Today the physical wall that divides our two communities is growing ever longer. And yet I believe that God has a plan for Israel and the Arab nations together. I believe our salvation is linked; it's a family matter. And God is in the business of healing and restoring families. He wants to heal this incredible breach not just between Israel and the nations but particularly between Israel and the Arab nations. Isaiah 19 describes this in detail. The world needs to see and know that Y'shua/Jesus came from the Father, and the only way we've been given to express this is by our love for each other and our unity in Messiah. This unity is not abstract theory – it has to be seen that we love one another and that we walk together in unity.

'Politically there are no answers. People need to talk and listen and let go of agendas. I look to the grass-roots, people meeting people, incremental building. But I believe the structures can be affected at one level. Prayer is a powerful tool for God to use, as we intercede and pray with and for one another for the common good, for the vision that we can see together. I don't see Islam as the horrible enemy. I see Islam as a religion that is used by the forces of darkness in this world, but Muslims are people for whom Y'shua died as well. There are a growing number of MBBs (Muslim-background believers) in the West Bank in Israel today, and it's important that the gospel penetrates these people at a grass-roots level. I understand there are tens of thousands of MBBs worldwide – people are coming into a saving knowledge of Y'shua as Lord from a Muslim background. It's happening here and it's a movement that is gaining momentum.'

I was interested that Lisa didn't describe Islam as being the dark spiritual force and number-one enemy that perhaps many Christians in the West would describe it as.

'I see it as one of many factors, but perhaps not the most crucial factor here. In my opinion, the most crucial factors in the fight for Israel's soul today are internal corruption and secularism. These internal threats are greater than the outside threat of Islam. But it's easier to focus on the outside threat. Nations of the world know this and so do leaders. The enemy from within destroys far more effectively than the enemy from without. Every time there is a security threat the people will coalesce and pull together. But when that threat is removed or reduced, then the internal problems surface – and we have a lot of them in this country today. At the same time, we believe that God is moving in Israel and He is putting Israel in a place where we have nowhere else to turn except to Him. I see it as His love. His judgment is always redemptive and as He's manoeuvring the forces of history and the affairs of the world, Israel is increasingly isolated from the community of nations and being criticized, sometimes for very good reasons. Is God moving in this or is He not? Is He in control? Of course He is. So what is He doing? He's bringing us to the point where we have nowhere else to turn but to Him. We cannot turn to politics. We cannot turn to religion. We have to turn to God.'

I felt Lisa was describing a spectrum of spirituality in Israel ranging from the very needy and lost to those who are spiritually alive and are even looking beyond Israel to reaching the other nations.

'Yes,' she agreed, 'and part of what I've devoted my life to, particularly in recent times, has been leadership development, because we're seeing a new generation of leaders coming up in this country. David and I are the grandparents. Then there's a younger generation. But then there's an even younger generation coming up now, and our heart is to resource and equip and release this younger generation – and they are an entirely different breed of people.

'In my work with Caspari [a Messianic research organization], I had four years of involvement in leadership development. We kept it small because we could only accommodate twenty-five students each year. But in that group of twenty-five students we had native-born Israelis, Russian immigrants, Ethiopian immigrants, Arab Christians and Anglo-Saxon immigrants. It was multigenerational, included men and women, and was a microcosm of the Body of Messiah, the body of faith in this country, all learning together. Now their studies were important, of course. But what was just as important was the interaction between the people and the breaking down of prejudices. We were building an infrastructure of relationships for the future in addition to equipping them with tools for conflict resolution, vision building, pastoral care and stress management – all very practical issues for leaders. But what God was doing was just as important as the curriculum!

'I think it's so important for the church in the West not to become polarized. In some places there are very pro-Israel Zionist Christians and very active pro-Palestinian segments of the church, and unfortunately when you identify yourself as pro- something, the counterpart to that is that you're anti- something else. And I think as Christians, or as believers in Messiah, we cannot afford to be anti-. We must be pro-Messiah and understand that He is working and moving amongst the Jewish people and amongst the Arab people. We encourage Christians worldwide to support the work of God; to see where the Holy Spirit is moving and support that work. The Holy Spirit is alive and moving in Gaza. The Holy Spirit is alive and moving in the Palestinian Territories. And for sure, the Holy Spirit is alive and moving in Israel, and I don't think we have to choose to support one and be against the other.'

Lisa had shared her understanding of Israel's destiny with me, and now it was time for her to leave for a meeting in Jerusalem – a gathering of international church leaders who would be discussing many of these questions together.

It was time to talk to Lisa's husband, David.

He seemed almost reticent to talk about what God might or might not be doing; such matters, he believed, were way beyond his understanding. It's important to realize that David Loden is a gentle and humble man. He's quiet but passionate about his faith. He's passionate too about Israel. He's passionate that the Body of Messiah in Israel should understand her destiny and 'get it right'. Slowly and cautiously he began to share his thoughts...

'I think there's a groundswell of change starting in this country amongst the younger generation – people in their late teens to late twenties. So over the next year or two I expect to see wonderful things happening in that area. Young people in this country are bursting with enthusiasm and with desires and dreams and ambitions, because they're young people and that's what young people do. They are like young plants bursting to produce flowers and move forward. Previous channels for that creativity and energy have proven to be false trails – unfounded dreams that have shattered. I'm speaking particularly about philosophies, politics and an idealistic approach to living in this country.

'So I think that as the Lord begins to move amongst His people He will, as it were, take the cap off, and that energy and desire for life will be reflected in a move towards salvation. I think it's a groundswell that will start with young people, but as it grows it will bring with it many more sectors of the population. The country is full of people who have zeal for God but lack of knowledge. I expect to see young people from the orthodox religious establishment, particularly the ultra-orthodox, included in this. I think there was a time when we looked upon them as enemies because they so diligently stood against us – they still do, in fact, and they harass us because of our beliefs. And yet they, in their own way, are looking for the missing piece of this puzzle, which is the Messiah Himself. So as this starts to happen in the country, I think there's going to be a tremendous move amongst the ultra-orthodox people. I won't stretch out and say what I think the results of that will be for the country, because I think it will bring tremendous turmoil and tremendous divisions.

'The young people are very happy to sit down and talk to you today about spiritual matters. Ten years ago people were very hedonistic and they didn't want to hear such things. The older generation was very conservative in their antagonism towards the faith. But now there is a new openness, particularly amongst young people, and I think there will be a move towards the Lord by them and orthodox people too. It will bring division. The Lord said He came not to bring peace but to bring a sword – a separation between those who will hear His voice and those who will not. When we came to the Lord in the midst of the hippie movement, along with many others who were together with us in that lifestyle, and we began to share what the Lord had shown us and how we came to know Him, it literally divided the camp right down the middle so that half went off in anger that we would betray them in this way, while the other half were quite open to listen. So half is a good number! And many of those people came to know the Lord. I am amazed there are so many congregational leaders in Israel today who came out of the hippie movement in the mid sixties. Many of those people who had dropped out of society were alternative people then, so there is a tremendous similarity to the situation today. Many of those hippies were Jews and so we find them today in the Body. The alternative people of today are truly creative in trying to find a blending of an innate understanding that God exists with a desire to demonstrate that fact in a practical way, especially in the area of social action.

'Young people of today are coming to faith more quickly than people of my generation; I'm talking about those born and raised in this country, because the issue of identity is quite different for an Israeli Jew compared with a Jew in the Diaspora. A Jewish person outside of Israel lives in a world that is not his own, a world that is antagonistic to his views and in which he has to struggle to maintain his identity and traditions. Here in Israel they don't have that struggle.'

David and Lisa spend much of their time with young believers, so I was interested to ask how these young Messianic Jews view their destiny in relation to Israel's destiny.

'Generally they are open and determined that they are going to be salt and light in the land. The young believers amongst the Messianic Body in Israel are tremendously active in Israel, pregnant with ideas, and their numbers and spiritual development are growing rapidly. My fear is that the other people in the congregations are not growing at the same rate; they are more conservative and can drag their feet, and so we are seeing the young people becoming quite frustrated.'

Would it be true to say their parents' generation would confine themselves to their local situation, whereas the young people are realizing there is a bigger picture, a greater destiny?

'Yes, I think that as far as the average young Israeli believer is concerned, he understands he has a part to play in the larger body of believers worldwide. They may struggle to define what that part is, but there is a very clear sense of calling that they need to be a part of this. Some of it comes from looking at the Scriptures through new eyes – reading the Hebrew Scriptures through Hebrew eyes. And so they understand their destiny in relation to Israel being "a light to the nations". As a matter of fact we are already seeing it. We've got young people from our congregations in Israel who are now all over the world. It's small and not well supported yet. In our congregation here in Netanya we are committed to seeing that "the

Word shall go forth from Zion";[5] we are sending groups of young people to Germany and Holland. For the past couple of years we've been sending a team of five young people from the congregation to the Ukraine, and we have numbers of people who travel abroad on speaking tours. So it's already begun.'

CHAPTER 4

Claude Ezagouri

It was time to leave Netanya and travel north to Tiberias, which is situated on the south-western shore of the Sea of Galilee. I would be back in Netanya to meet with Evan Thomas the next day, but first I had to meet two Messianic pastors in the north, Claude Ezagouri and Daniel Yahav.

It was time to take a bus ride! David Loden very kindly drove me out of Netanya to the Beit Lid junction where, I was assured, a bus would arrive in a few minutes' time. This junction is situated out of town on a major crossroads and I felt I was in the middle of nowhere. Sitting under a bus shelter on an island surrounded by busy traffic, I waited along with a young female soldier. She was pacing up and down, looking at her watch. It was the middle of the day, and the temperature was soaring. On the other side of the road was a van selling drinks and sandwiches. I thought about crossing over to buy some lunch, but thought better of it. I was working to a tight schedule; I couldn't afford to miss the bus for a sandwich!

Eventually the bus arrived and I climbed on board. It was an interesting journey. Bearing north, we turned right at Hadera and proceeded to cross the Yizre'el Valley, past Megido towards Afula. This vast plain stretches for many miles; plenty of time to think about Armageddon. I saw the road running north to Nazareth and shortly afterwards Mount Tabor came into view. This dome-shaped mountain sits on the flat plain like a lump of dough; it's an incongruous site and quite unmistakable. Memories of Deborah and Sisera flashed through my mind. That's the thing about travelling through the land of Israel: Bible stories come alive and run through your mind like a movie. Real places where real people lived and died, but not before they'd left a lasting impression; voices from the past capable of speaking into our modern situation.

Then we started the descent towards Tiberias. The Sea of Galilee, which forms part of the Rift Valley, lies 207 metres below sea level. The water is fresh and provides Israel with half its water supply. Tiberias is the largest city in Galilee and dates back 2,000 years to the Romans – indeed, it was named after the Roman Emperor Tiberius.

Eventually the bus pulled into the central bus station at Tiberias and after getting my suitcase out of the luggage hold, I walked through the busy, jostling town to my hotel.

By this time it was late afternoon and the sun was beginning to set, casting its light across the lake to the Golan Heights beyond, which glowed pink. With the mist of morning long gone, this is always a good time to see the far-reaching views across the lake. Nothing much has changed here. I think that's why people love being around the Sea of Galilee – it is largely unspoilt and for the Christian, it's thrilling to take a Bible and use it as a guidebook in tracing the steps of Jesus in this region. Capernaum, Korazim, Bethsaida… you can visit them all and recall what happened there.

But I was here to find out what is happening in Tiberias today. Later that evening Claude Ezagouri came to meet me at the hotel. He and his wife, Michelle, were both born in Algeria. After living in France for many years, they came to Israel in 1975. Today Claude is the Pastor of the Morning Star Fellowship in Tiberias.

'We started the ministry seventeen years ago,' he told me in his heavy French accent.

'You're one of the pioneers,' I replied. 'Why did you come to Tiberias?'

Claude and Michelle's story reveals a long search. I always find Jewish people from Arab countries extremely interesting because their journey, both physical and spiritual, appears to take them through many experiences. In Claude's case, he came through Judaism to faith in Y'shua as his Messiah via Hinduism and Transcendental Meditation; in fact he devoted so much time to meditation that he almost wrecked their marriage. It was through a book given to him by his wife that Claude became a believer – a book about meditating on the words of Jesus! And two years later, Michelle too became convinced. Their marriage was saved and their life together continued – but in a completely different direction.

'We used to live in a *kibbutz* and in 1989 the Lord spoke to me very clearly one night. I heard His voice telling me some surprising things. He talked of us leaving the *kibbutz* and He promised to bless us. I had to ask for confirmation; I was very afraid – but I was convinced by the Lord that I had to move from the *kibbutz* and settle in Tiberias. I didn't know why at the time. But we came here and about one and a half years later the Lord called me into the ministry. He confirmed this to me with signs and wonders, so if there's one thing I'm sure of, it's that I'm called to do what I'm doing!'

'What was your vision in those early days?' I asked.

'To begin with I didn't see the whole picture. Then on 14 July 1990 the Lord said to me, "Start a congregation and start to evangelize." At that time there were a lot of Jews coming to Israel from the former USSR and we soon realized that it was very easy to talk to them about Y'shua! We would share our faith and people would cry and receive the Lord one after another, and within a few weeks we had a full house. The Lord was doing wonderful things. It was much later that He started to give me the first pieces of the puzzle about the vision. So for many years we worked hard with the fellowship, making many mistakes along the way, which taught us a lot. We continued with evangelism and teaching and doing what we were supposed to do, although not fully understanding where the Lord was leading us.

'However, I was profoundly moved by two stories, one from Luke's Gospel (Luke 5: 1–11) and the other from John's Gospel (John 21:1–14). Both had to do with fishing and nets. The main difference between the two miraculous fishing stories is that in the second one the nets did not tear. The Lord showed me that I was to start to repair the nets today.

'At first I didn't know how the Lord wanted me to do this. However, shortly afterwards the fellowship met for a night of prayer and during the night the Lord showed us a net and said, "Make disciples and invest in people who will be the net with which you will catch the fish. The fish will be ready on the right-hand side of the boat." And so I believe that what will happen – and the Lord has confirmed this to me several times since – is that as we continue to evangelize, we will see that the people are ready to receive Y'shua, just as on the right-hand side of the boat the fish were there ready to be caught. The only thing they needed was a net. And that's what I feel about Israel. The fish are ready. And we see some evidence of this already – the first fruits of the harvest. There are people who say, "I feel that I'm attracted to Jesus", or "I had a dream about Jesus", or "I don't understand what's happening but I'm open to that". So there is some evidence that the Lord is preparing the people's hearts and He will send the fish. We, in turn, will have to know how to process the fish; we have to be ready to welcome them – and this is the work we are engaged with right now and this is where I am trying to invest my strength and my knowledge and my prayers. How do I build nets that will bring the fish home? We don't want a repeat of the first miraculous fishing where the nets broke; I guess it's not the dream of any fisherman to know the fish are there but he can't catch them because his nets are torn. What the Lord wants is for all those He has prepared to come home.

'Recently the Lord has really sharpened the vision in my mind; He started to speak to me about the base we would have in downtown Tiberias. To tell you the truth, I thought at first that we needed to have a building on the edge of town. The Lord gave us many instances of people passing by the Church of Scotland, where we meet, who heard worship in Hebrew and were attracted and came in. But when they saw it was a church, complete with a cross on the wall, they left. When we talked to them they said they were really attracted by the music and the worship, but couldn't understand why we met in a church building. We tried to explain that we are Messianic Jews and not Christians but they still said, "But you are in a church." What they meant was, "Our problem is, you're in a [Gentile Christian] church building – otherwise we would join you, because we like what you're doing. But the fact that you're in a church is a stumbling-block for us." And we understand their problem, because when we look back on 2,000 years of Christian persecution of the Jews, for them the cross represents the sword of the Crusaders. Many Christians don't understand this, but we do here.

'Then during our prayer meetings the Lord told us, "I'm going to give you a building that will be a base to do what I gave you as a vision for this area – I want you downtown." I thought, *Wait a minute – this is quite another ball-game! Downtown means persecution, it means being in the heart of the turmoil.* Tiberias is a religious city. I thought they would never receive us downtown. And I spent a lot of time in prayer trying to convince God that He didn't know the situation in Tiberias and this was not a good idea! But the Lord said to me, "I am not only the God of the hills but also the God of the valleys." And downtown Tiberias is in a valley which stretches from the north, through the Dead Sea, and down to Eilat in the south.

'And so we started to look for a suitable building. At first we couldn't find anywhere, until one day we received a word from the Holy Spirit through an unbeliever. I knew it was the Lord's voice because we knew where the right place was, and this was exactly what we were looking for. As soon as we agreed to go ahead with this building, we started to have a lot of opposition; by now it was early 2005. Some rabbis started to interfere and put pressure on the owners of the building, and the door closed to us. A few months later, the door opened again;

then closed again. This continued for two years. I would pray, "Lord, you tell us this is the building, but you keep closing the door, so what are you doing?" And He gave me two words, one to me directly and one to my wife. He said to me, "I will break through the bronze gate," and to my wife, "I will open a door that no one can close." And He did! Suddenly I received a phone call from the owner who said, "No problem, you can come and we'll talk about it." So now the door is open, but that doesn't mean it's easy. We're still trying to work out this transaction, but I believe it will happen because the Lord has shown me that the building is a means for Him to accomplish what He wants.

'Looking to the future here in Israel, what I see is that it's getting darker and more violent. We see corruption in high circles. The Israeli people are frustrated and disappointed. What they are looking for is a group of people they can trust. They've tried everything. They've tried politics and it didn't work. Today, if you ask the average Israeli who they trust in government, they reply, "Nobody; we don't put our hope in politics." I believe that the Lord is creating an opportunity for the believers to speak up. And the challenge to us is for the Israeli people to be able to find the Lord through us. People know that believers have a good reputation. They know that we pay our taxes. They know that we don't cheat or lie. They know that we have a moral code. But the big question is, will we stick to this or will we disappoint them? It's a big challenge. I sometimes wonder if I can do it. Then I remember that it's God's work; He will do it. And so the Lord is giving the congregations an opportunity to show the people that we are here and that we want to bless the community in practical ways and demonstrate the love of

Y'shua to the Jewish community here.

'What would Y'shua do if He were here today? He would heal. He would deliver people who are oppressed. He would help them. And we have the opportunity to do this – maybe in a small measure to start with. Surely the Lord will open the door wide for us. We want to give people the opportunity to see who we are. Of course, for the first few months they will probably continue to accuse us of being "missionaries". But if we keep going with perseverance and faithfulness, maybe after one or two years, people will say, "Well, we may not like their Messiah, but what we see is good fruit." Actually, I am sure they will say, "If we have to choose people to be in the government, we will choose those Messianic believers." If we are to fulfil what the Lord is showing us, we need to act not only behind closed doors in our congregation but also outside on the streets of downtown Tiberias.

'We have to be bold. What we will do, we will do publicly. They will know who we are. It will be in the local media and press. It will be open because we will work in the midst of this community.

'In order for these things to happen, I believe there is going to be an outpouring of the Holy Spirit. In Romans 11 Paul describes this spiritual awakening in Israel as being like "life from the dead".[1] There is going to be a spiritual awakening in Israel that will make an impact on the world and on the church in the nations. We have the verse in Zechariah which says:

> This is what the Lord Almighty says: 'In
> those days ten men from all languages and
> nations will take firm hold of one Jew by
> the hem of his robe and say, "Let us go with

> you, because we have heard that God is
> with you."'[2]

'How will they hear that God is with Jews? Because of the outpouring of the Holy Spirit. The glory of God will be revealed. I don't know how. Maybe not as it was in the past. Maybe in a new way. But it will have an impact on the church in the nations, and many Gentiles will realize that God is doing something amongst the Jewish people, and they will want to come and be part of it. They will find a Jewish believer and pull his clothes. This is when I believe there will be complete cooperation between Messianic Jews and the church worldwide; they will understand and there will be heart-to-heart fellowship – something that we've longed to have for many years but which has eluded us because of the prevalence of Replacement Theology. The evil one knows that the Lord wants to see a merging of the church in the nations and the believers in Israel; and in some nations this is already happening. Even in a Muslim nation like Indonesia, there are thousands of believers who pray for Israel and invest in Israel. They will tell you that they didn't just decide to do this; rather, it was the Lord who revealed these things to them. And so it's spreading.

'As leaders of the Messianic community here in Israel, we are looking to the church worldwide. We want to present this message to the church in the nations and ask them to go to prayer and ask the Lord, "What do you want us to do with this new phenomenon called Messianic Jews in Israel?" We want them to try and understand what the Lord is saying. But there's still a lot of work to be done in this area.

'Recently I was speaking at a conference in

Europe and found myself amongst leaders of churches and Christian organizations gripped by Replacement Theology. At the beginning I had a hard time – it was like breaking ice. However, I quickly realized a difference in attitude between the majority of Christian leaders and the ordinary Christian people who were present. As I showed them the Scriptures and explained what the Lord is doing right now in Israel amongst the Jewish people, the ordinary Christians were very interested and said, "We've never been taught this and we want to know more. Come to our church. We want your newsletter!" But the problem was, their leaders didn't want them to know. There is so much work to do in the nations that it's almost becoming a dilemma. I am asking myself, how much time should I spend in Israel, and how much time abroad? Of course, my first priority is here, but I understand also that part of our call is to go to the nations, to those that have ears, and tell them this is what the Lord is saying. And I tell you it is so rewarding when people open their eyes; it's rewarding to see the results and see the fruit. Sometimes it's more rewarding than being here in Israel!'

Claude may have had a hard time persuading some Christian leaders, but clearly what he had to say was received enthusiastically by many individual Christians. I found it interesting that whilst the eyes of many in the church are being opened to see what God is doing in Israel, at the same time ordinary Israelis are also beginning to turn their attention to the growing numbers of Messianic believers in their midst. Is this merely a coincidence? Claude had told me earlier that in the next five to ten years he is anticipating an outpouring of the Holy Spirit in Israel, that God's power is going to be evident in signs and wonders and many are going to come into the Kingdom.

'Yes,' he said, 'and as the church in the nations comes in and identifies with the believers here, the Jewish people will see that after 2,000 years the Christians are no longer the enemies of the Jews. And as Christians receive this love for Israel, the Jews will be at first surprised, but when they see the genuine love it will be a testimony to them, and the first thing they will say is, "I don't know what's going on but there's a change in the air. You love us. Why?" There is a shift today in the spiritual realm, and I hope it's being understood by the church in the nations. For 2,000 years they considered the whole world as a mission field, including Israel. Well, let's face it, they were very successful in many nations, but they failed here. But now there is a shift. A shift that takes us back 2,000 years. What was the situation then? Missionaries went from Israel to the nations. And this is what the church in the nations needs to understand. Today there is something they need to receive from Israel that is for their benefit. They need to understand what the Lord is doing here today and that there is an open door for them to come in and be a part of it.

'There's a lot the church can do for Israel, not only in prayer and finances but in practical ways too. For example, there is a man I know who is a pastor in France and for years he has encouraged his congregation to pray for the salvation of Israel. One day the Lord said to him and his wife, "I want you for a time, for a season, to go to Israel." And do you know what the Lord asked them to do in Israel? He asked them to serve. So they worked in a hospital as cleaners. They helped the elderly. Many pastors would go to Israel to preach; not many would go and work in this humble way. But the Lord told him to serve the Jewish people in this way. When I saw this, I thought, what maturity this Christian pastor has, to come and show to the Jews that he is ready to do jobs that not even the Jews are prepared to do for each other, because he loves them. When the Jews see this they understand that something is happening and they ask, "Why are you doing this for us? We have never experienced this kind of love from Christians."'

I was interested to hear how the new believers in Claude's congregation interpret those scriptures that talk about Israel being a 'light to the nations'.[3] As well as being concerned to reach their own people with the gospel, are they now starting to turn outwards and look to fulfil that aspect of Israel's destiny?

'Yes, this is becoming clearer and clearer. We want to fulfil the call of Israel to the nations and this is the time. We have the verse that says, "In days to come Jacob will take root, Israel will bud and blossom and fill all the world with fruit."[4] And we ask ourselves this question: What is this fruit? Messianic Jews realize more and more that we're coming to a time when the Lord is saying that we have something to bring to the church, and at the same time many in the church are saying to us that they believe there is something we have to give to them. The church and Israel complete each other and they are the devil's nightmare. The enemy knows this well.'

CHAPTER 5

Daniel Yahav

The son of a Holocaust survivor from Germany, Daniel Yahav was born in Jaffa in 1959. He is the father of seven children, one of whom is adopted. He's a reserve major in the Israeli army. A former businessman, he is now the 'Servant' Pastor of the Peniel Fellowship in Tiberias.

We agreed to meet at eight o'clock the following morning. I'd been up early and walked around the edge of the Sea of Galilee in front of the Caesar Hotel in Tiberias where I had spent the night. I'd never met Daniel before. In fact I'd never heard of him; he deliberately keeps a low profile – his story reveals why.

He pulled up in front of the hotel in a large white van which looked like it had covered many miles and was used for carrying people and goods on a regular basis. 'Let me show you a few places in Tiberias,' he said, and with that we drove out of the hotel grounds.

'Over there is our school,' he said, pointing to a black-and-white stone building. 'It's run by the congregation and we have thirty children there.'

We drove up a hill through an old quarter of Tiberias. 'There's our kindergarten and clothing centre.'

Then a little further on, he slowed down as we passed

a house, a former hotel. 'That's where we used to live and where we started the congregation, until the orthodox Jews drove us out by their continual attacks – breaking windows, throwing stones, and eventually setting fire to the place.'

Daniel was setting the scene! Life as a pastor in Tiberias clearly had its challenges. 'We met in the open countryside for five years before eventually finding this building.' We had driven into a small industrial site on the outskirts of Tiberias. Climbing out of the van, we heard an alarm ringing.

'Not again!' muttered Daniel. 'Sounds like we've had visitors.' Without flinching, he unlocked the sturdy iron door, turned off the alarm, switched on all the lights and walked in to see what had happened. I followed him cautiously. Daniel checked the building and found that nothing was untoward. He breathed a sigh of relief.

As I looked around the inside of what, on the outside, looked like a factory unit, I realized with what care and attention to detail Daniel Yahav and his congregation had transformed and adapted this building. The main auditorium seated approximately 300. 'We've already outgrown this place,' he told me. There was a large kitchen with a serving hatch into the reception area. There were folding doors between the auditorium and the reception to create an even larger open space. 'We have to open this area up every week,' Daniel added. Down another corridor there were some smaller rooms. 'We have so many children now, they need somewhere to meet.'

I sensed I was somewhere special and anticipated that the story I was about to hear would demonstrate the essence of what God is doing in Israel today, as well as what He is going to do in the future to fulfil Israel's destiny, in making her a light to the nations, as predicted in the Scriptures.

As we sat down to record the interview, it was obvious that Daniel was ready and well prepared.

'When you look at Isaiah's prophecy about Israel being a light, it has primarily been fulfilled through Jesus and the disciples and the Messianic Jewish believers in the early church who went out and spread the light to the nations. However, it also has a present and a future fulfilment.

'At the present time, I can tell you from personal experience what the Lord is doing here amongst us Jews. As we study the Old Testament with our knowledge of Hebrew, living in this land and with the Holy Spirit as our teacher, we discover things in the Old Testament – shadows of Jesus and His crucifixion – which have been hidden from the church worldwide for a number of reasons. One reason is that the church cut itself off from its roots. Another reason is that the translations of the Bible from Hebrew to other languages failed to reveal these things. To me these "shadows" are like diamonds that have been lying in a field covered with dust, and you have to remove the "dust" of these other translations. I don't blame the translators, because the Hebrew language is so condensed, often they have had to interpret rather than translate the text. You realize this when you compare the number of Hebrew words with the number of, say, English words. Take any verse of the Bible and count the number of Hebrew words and count the number of English words, and you will find there are often 50 per cent more English words. This is because the Old Testament Hebrew text is so rich that the interpreter has to choose the best words he can to convey the meaning. They've done a very good job but it shows the limitation of translations.

'And so, for example, we find Jesus on the road to Emmaus talking with the two disciples. He was explaining to them, drawing from the writings of Moses, about events that had just taken place that week in Jerusalem. "Beginning with Moses and all the Prophets, he explained to them what was said in all the Scriptures concerning himself."[1] Now, what do you find in Moses about His crucifixion? Well, there are a number of pictures of His cross; for example: "So Moses made a bronze snake and put it on a pole. Then when anyone was bitten by a snake and looked at the bronze snake, he lived."[2] The Lord Himself compared His cross to the pole on which the snake was put.

'And there are other wonderful pictures that are still hidden. Some are prophetic; they have not all been fulfilled. There are still shadows that have yet to be fulfilled. So the Old Testament is very relevant – it's not out of date. Some people think that because we have the New Testament we don't need the Old Testament. But when you study the Old Testament and put it next to the New Testament, they enrich each other. By the way, by studying the Old Testament we are not bringing people under the Law – this has nothing to do with that. The New Testament quotes the Old hundreds of times. You can't fully understand the New without the Old.

'As for Israel being a light to the nations, firstly, when I travel abroad and meet with Christians in other nations, I see a growing hunger in people who want to know more about the roots of their faith. There is a big danger when Christian people try to go back to the roots of their faith and end up in Rabbinical Judaism – that is not our root!

'Jesus Himself warned against this approach in His parable when he told His disciples to be wary of the "yeast" of the Pharisees and Sadducees.[3] This could lead to the same confusion we read about in the book of Acts,[4] when Jewish believers came out of Jerusalem and tried to bring Christians [i.e. Gentiles] back under the Law – which you read about in Paul's letter to the Galatians, for example. Sadly, we see the same thing happening today. So when I talk about our roots, I don't talk about Rabbinical Judaism; I talk about the light we have in the Old Testament, the Bible, the living Word of God!

'The second way Israel is yet to be a light to the nations is when the 144,000 Jewish witnesses that we read about in the book of Revelation will go out. You can imagine the impact they will have on this dark and evil world in the last days.

'However, there is a third aspect in which Israel is to be a light to the nations, a very important one which is greatly misunderstood and not acknowledged by some Christians. This aspect concerns the physical rebirth of the State of Israel.

'You see, God has got a master plan to sanctify His name among all the nations of the earth. This is to be done through the regathering of the nation of Israel to its land and through the end-time wars.

'Allow me to explain. Light is seen whenever God reveals Himself and brings people to acknowledge Him. So it can come in a pleasant way – God can send fishermen who entice you with bait and tell you Jesus is good, He loves you and gave His life for you. Or it can come through the hunters – through wars, through difficult times.

'God says in Ezekiel:

> Therefore say to the house of Israel, 'This is
> what the Sovereign Lord says: It is not for
> your sake, O house of Israel, that I am going
> to do these things, but for the sake of my
> holy name, which you have profaned among
> the nations where you have gone. I will
> show the holiness of my great name, which
> has been profaned among the nations, the
> name you have profaned among them.
> Then the nations will know that I am the
> Lord, declares the Sovereign Lord, when I
> show myself holy through you before their
> eyes.'[5]

'Through Israel's sin and through God's need to punish us and send us into exile, we as a nation have defiled God's name. You see, when we went into the nations, we became a mockery and the scum of the earth. Our enemies likened us to rats, as we saw in Hitler's time – sub-human. Yet we were the chosen nation of God and God's name was upon us still, even in our rebellion. In this way we brought shame on the name of God. Yet He says that He will sanctify His holy name. In Ezekiel 36 – 39, God reveals His plan of action. It starts where God declares that He will gather Israel back to their land: "For I will take you out of the nations. I will gather you from all the countries and bring you back into your own land."[6]

'This re-gathering, which started at the end of the nineteenth century, marked the beginning of the conflict in the Middle East. The devil has used religious and nationalistic spirits to provoke enmity against Israel in order to try and destroy her. It starts when the nations surrounding Israel[7] come to war against her but fail, and it will continue with all the nations[8] coming against Jerusalem to attack her. These nations will be destroyed by Y'shua Himself when He returns.[9]

'The prophet Jeremiah calls these wars the "tribulation of Jacob".[10] It will be a fire of tribulation for us as a nation. Two thirds living in the land will perish in these wars.[11] "'In the whole land,' declares the Lord, 'two-thirds will be struck down and perish; yet one-third will be left in it.'"

'God's relationship to His people will be restored. Y'shua will be revealed to us[12] and we will repent. As this takes place, God's name will be sanctified [i.e. made holy] in our midst. Our sin, which defiled His name, will be burnt out from among us.

'Then God will deal with the rebellious nations of the world. Y'shua will come from heaven and utterly destroy them. There are many passages of Scripture dealing with this phase. Zechariah 14:12–15, Isaiah 63:1–6 and Ezekiel 38 – 39 are just a few.

'In Ezekiel we read about Gog and Magog coming against Israel. Here is a clear description of how God uses these wars to sanctify His name:

> You will come from your place in the far
> north, you and many nations with you, all
> of them riding on horses, a great horde, a
> mighty army. You will advance against my
> people Israel like a cloud that covers the
> land. In days to come, O Gog, I will bring
> you against my land, so that the nations may
> know me when I show myself holy through
> you before their eyes.[13]

'God says:

> I will summon a sword against Gog on
> all my mountains, declares the Sovereign
> Lord. Every man's sword will be against
> his brother. I will execute judgement upon
> him with plague and bloodshed. I will
> pour down torrents of rain, hailstones and
> burning sulphur on him and on his troops
> and on the many nations with him. And so
> I will show my greatness and my holiness,
> and I will make myself known in the sight
> of many nations. Then they will know that I
> am the Lord.[14]

'Gog and Magog will start fighting each other. God will judge them with "plague and bloodshed" and "hailstones", until finally the nations will come to realize that "I am God." So we understand God's master-plan, that through these wars involving Israel, He will bring "the light" to the nations – then they will know that He is the Lord.

'The unrest we experience today is fuelled by the anti-Israel stance taken by many in the media who report that Israelis are aggressors who don't want peace. This is the same anti-Semitism or anti-Israelism, but in a different form, which will eventually lead to the coming of the anti-Christ who will lead his armies to invade Israel. But through these calamites, and through the destruction of these armies, and through the punishment that will fall on the nations, eventually the nations will come to understand that the God of Israel is the true God.[15] God will bring this world to its knees through all of this – it is designed by God. No politician can bring about a lasting peace here. A false, temporary peace will come, but indeed there will not be a lasting peace because the Bible talks about these wars with the nations surrounding Israel[16] that will eventually involve the rest of the world:[17] "the nations will know that I am the Lord, declares the Sovereign Lord, when I show myself holy through you before their eyes."

'However, we need to understand that God has a master-plan for making His name holy. His name is being defiled among the nations today. Europe, that used to be Christian Europe, has become pagan Europe. Born-again Christians are in the minority in European nations.

'The average Israeli wants peace. We are not aggressors, even though this is how we are portrayed. We don't want our sons to go into the army. We don't want them to have to fight and be killed. We just want peace like everybody else in the world. We're being hated; we have been hated in the past – all over Europe and throughout the Arab world. Our worst treatment was at the hands of the Europeans. My father was a Holocaust survivor. He went through Auschwitz. Most of his family was killed during the Holocaust.

'Those reading this book ought to know that today is the day to pray for the governments of the world. Today is the day to personally take the right side. And the right side is not standing with Israel. The right side is standing with God, understanding what He is doing and taking His side. Since He is the one who has brought Israel back to this land, then any force and any person who objects, anyone who divides up the land, is really dividing up God's land and is actually criticizing God's plans.'

Knowing the thoughts and opinions of many Christians in the UK on this subject, and given that this book is aimed at the church in the West, I asked Daniel to enlarge on this point. I reminded him that many Christians in Europe are antagonistic towards Israel, whilst others consider Israel an irrelevance compared to the mission of the church.

'Well, this reveals a fundamental lack of understanding of the Scriptures,' Daniel replied. 'I would say spiritual and theological pride is probably one of the main reasons for this blindness and misunderstanding. Once you become proud you are set for a fall. Replacement Theology is fundamentally flawed. Those Church Fathers who introduced this way of thinking are accountable before God for deceiving many, and today is the time for anyone who loves God and seeks His truth to recognize this error and search the Scriptures and see that God is committed to His covenant with Israel. He is committed to His promises; He is committed to His words, to everything He has said through the prophets. If God ever abandoned His covenants and His promises and His prophecies with Israel, what guarantee do we have as a church that He will remain faithful to us? Because of the sin of Israel, she has been totally rejected – so what about the sin of the church? What about the divisions in the church? What about the wars and the bloodshed that the church has been responsible for? What about the hypocrisy and the sin that is prevailing everywhere in the church? If the church claims to have the greater light, that they are the "chosen ones", then have they forgotten the words of Jesus, "From everyone who has been given much, much will be demanded; and from the one who has been entrusted with much, much more will be asked"?[18]

'Another key passage that I believe many in the church

fail to properly understand is in Matthew's Gospel,[19] where Jesus predicts the destruction of Jerusalem: "O Jerusalem, Jerusalem, you who kill the prophets and stone those sent to you, how often I have longed to gather your children together as a hen gathers her chicks under her wings, but you were not willing." Here we see how much God wanted to "gather" Israel, and this gives us an insight into the heart of God; this was always His intention. He's speaking with pain. In other passages we read how Jesus wept when he looked over Jerusalem. It was not an arrogant, hateful rejection or condemnation of Israel. The heart of God was to "gather Israel" but they would not allow Him to; as a result, "Look, your house is left to you desolate." Then Jesus said, "For I tell you, you will not see me again until you say, 'Blessed is he who comes in the name of the Lord.'"

'What does that mean? In the following chapter[20] Jesus says, "For as lightning that comes from the east is visible even in the west, so will be the coming of the Son of Man."

'In other words, everyone will see Him. So Jesus is saying, "You will not see me until you Jews call upon me and welcome me. Now you are rejecting me. Now you are sending me as a curse to the cross. As a result you will not see me, I will be hidden away from you until the day comes when you recognize me and call on me; only then will I come back." And when Jesus comes again, He will not come again in a hidden way like in His first advent; rather, He will come to the Mount of Olives, to Jerusalem. Heaven will open up as described in Revelation 19:11–16 and in Zechariah 14:3–4. This means Jesus will not come back and establish His physical Kingdom on earth (and it will be a physical kingdom and not just a theological concept) until we as a nation repent and come to know Him. How will that happen? The Holy Spirit will be poured upon us in the middle of these hard times during the wars. The prophet Zechariah says, "And I will pour out on the house of David and the inhabitants of Jerusalem a spirit of grace and supplication. They will look on me, the one they have pierced, and they will mourn for him as one mourns for an only child…"[21]

'So if the church wants to see the Kingdom of God established, if Christians really mean what they say when they pray, "Thy Kingdom come",[22] if we want to see His Kingdom come not just in the hearts of people but physically on earth, we have to realize that the condition for His Kingdom to come is the salvation of Israel. He will not come before Israel calls upon Him.

'I once visited the Cathedral of Strasbourg and there, at the entrance, stand two female statues representing the church (*Ecclesia*) and the synagogue (*Synagoga*). They date from AD 1230 and are stone witnesses revealing an attitude of Christian superiority about Judaism. *Ecclesia* is portrayed as a proud and victorious queen holding the symbols of victory in her hands – the cross and the cup of Communion – whereas *Synagoga* is shown with clear signs of defeat, her head bowed down, without a crown, a broken lance and the tablets of the law pointing downwards in her hands. This is a picture of the church elevating herself over and against Israel. Imagine the influence this must have had on people in the thirteenth century, most of whom would have been unable to read; and how this must have helped fuel the fire of anti-Semitism in the Middle Ages in Europe when the dominant culture was supposedly Christian. It's true, Israel has sinned and has been judged. However, God said to the Gentile church through Paul in Romans, "Do not boast".[23]

'And this is exactly what the church has done; she has boasted and elevated herself over and against Israel. A few verses later Paul says, "For if God did not spare the natural branches, he will not spare you either."[24] And let me tell you, the church in Europe is being cut off. It is losing ground. Churches are shutting down. The church is in retreat; it is blind, it is naked, it is poor, it is in a miserable condition and it does not even recognize it. It's like the church in Laodicea[25] who thought themselves rich and enlightened; they did not recognize they were poor and naked and miserable and blind. And yet, out of His love, Jesus calls them to repent:[26] "I counsel you to buy from me gold refined in the fire, so you can become rich; and white clothes to wear, so you can cover your shameful nakedness; and salve to put on your eyes, so you can see." So be earnest and repent.

'The church in Europe does have the chance to wake up. What does it mean to be purified by fire? Fire means tribulation. And if you really want to do something that will be of value in the Kingdom of God, it will cost you sacrificially; you will have to go through the fire. You will be criticized. But in this fire, you will start gathering yourself gold that will last. This is where you will prove your love for the Lord. And this is our experience here. And this will be your experience in Europe. The dormant church doesn't realize how the powers of darkness are gathering strength and momentum. I'm not a pessimist, but I see what the Word of God says. Persecution will come in the times of Anti-Christ, and his spirit is prevailing all over Europe. The church will be persecuted.

'Here's another thing the church has largely missed: the believers in Israel and the Christians in the rest of the world share the same God – the God of Israel.

We share the same destiny. One day we will be united because the prophet Zechariah clearly says, "In those days ten men from all languages and nations will take firm hold of one Jew by the hem of his robe and say, 'Let us go with you, because we have heard that God is with you.'"[27] You Gentiles have joined us in our blessings and promises. You have joined the household of God; so we have the same destiny and we also have the same enemy. Anti-Christ will persecute the Jews and the church. We as Israel are still blind. The church, which has the light, should have prayed for their older but blinder brother. Who else can pray for us? We must stand together. This 2,000-year-old "mistake" must stop. It's time for the church to wake up and take its stand on God's side and provoke us, Israel, to jealousy and stop criticizing us. If you stand on God's side, you'll be totally changed in your attitude towards Israel.

'The Body here in Israel is growing, not just in numbers. If I look at the youth in our congregation, I see their desire to live a holy life, to be committed to the Lord and serve Him by dedicating their lives to Him. There is a huge harvest yet to be gathered, a last ingathering from among the nations in places like China. And parallel to this last ingathering, we see how God is dealing with Israel – the state of Israel and then the body of believers here. First comes the physical then the spiritual awakening. My father was a dry bone that was brought out of Auschwitz and assembled here with all the other dry bones, and I, his son, have the privilege of being part of the spiritual revival of Israel. [See the two-phase restoration of Israel in Ezekiel 37:1–15.]

'I started attending an Israeli congregation in 1966 at the age of seven. There were very few Messianic believers then and the pastor who started the church was one of only a handful of Messianic Jews who lived here during the time of the War of Independence. His name was Haim Bar David – a Bulgarian Jew. He accepted the Lord in 1920 and came to Israel (Palestine as it then was called) in 1929. He was committed. He stuck here. He had seven children. He lived in Jerusalem and was persecuted by orthodox Jews and shot at by Arabs. Eventually he started a fellowship. It grew around his family, and that's where I came to faith.

'My father was very much against my faith and tried to talk me out of it. My mother and two sisters came to faith before I did and eventually they were baptized. Although I started going to the fellowship at a young age, I only committed my life to the Lord at the age of fifteen and took water baptism. A few years later I joined the army and served four years. I was a tank officer during one of the wars. I still serve in the army – I'm a major in the reserves.

'When I first started walking with the Lord at the age of fifteen, I made a commitment and surrendered my life to the Lord. It was deep, wholehearted, real – there was never any turning back. At the time I was alone, there was no youth group, and I was in a small fellowship. My nearest friend in age was five years older than me. The Body of Messiah was so small in those days that when we had a national youth camp in the summer, there were maybe thirty teenagers! At that time I never envisaged that one day I would be leading a congregation. In fact, I had no inclination to be a leader. I married whilst in the army; I met my wife in a Messianic youth camp. I married when I was twenty-one; she was seventeen. When we married in 1980, we invited all the believers in Israel –

we all knew each other at that time. We had almost 200 guests at our wedding! And they came from all corners of the land.

'As soon as I came out of the army, I spent three days in prayer and fasting and asked the Lord where He wanted me to be. I had no preconceived plans or ideas. Instead of directing me to go to university, He gave me the desire to find a job where I would be working with believers who began the day with prayer. I did not know of such a business. It was 1981 and the Body of Messiah was still very small. I felt led to come and live in Tiberias, and shortly after we moved here I met an American Christian brother called Ken who owned a factory here. He invited me for an interview and when I heard they started every morning with prayer, I knew that was the place the Lord had prepared for me. Indeed, I told him I was coming to work for him! I didn't ask him about the kind of work he wanted me to do. I just said, "I'm coming!" He wanted to tell me how much I'd be earning and I said, "I'll see it when I get my first payslip – no problem!" I was convinced that was where God wanted me.

'So I started at the back of the factory as a production worker for Galtronics. God blessed the work and in 1985 I was appointed the Director General Manager of the company. At that time Galtronics was a small and struggling company with about thirty workers. We were producing antennas for hand-held radios. We had great financial difficulties – actually the company almost went bankrupt. We cried out to the Lord and He heard our prayers. He led us into the unknown and emerging cellular market. We were the first company to design and later manufacture antennas, and by 1990 Galtronics had become the largest manufacturer in the world of antennas for the cellular market, holding an estimated 70 per cent of the market. We paid off all our debts and expanded from a 300-square-metre plant to a 5,400-square-metre plant, with two factories in Israel, one in the UK (which was later transferred to China), and sales offices in the US. It was a real success. The government of Israel honoured us with the Israeli Kaplan prize, awarded to us at the Israeli Knesset in Jerusalem. Praise the Lord!

'While the business was growing, the fellowship was also growing. In 1992 we had two elders – Ken, who was also the President of Galtronics, and me. We were both very busy with the company and were asking God how He wanted us to handle the fellowship. It was obvious we needed a full-time pastor.

'Early one morning, as I was waking up, the Lord spoke to me and said I was to leave the company and become the full-time pastor of the congregation. He showed me the full scenario and it was incredible, because part of the plan was that the company would continue to pay my salary for a period of time!

'Two days after the Lord spoke to me, I met with Ken for our regular weekly elders' meeting. All of a sudden he said, "Daniel, you know the situation with the fellowship. How would you feel about becoming the full-time pastor for one year? We'll pay your salary. And we'll keep your position open at Galtronics – I won't hire anybody in place of you. And then we'll bring you back in." This was exactly what the Lord had shown me. It was incredible!

'To encourage us and affirm that this was indeed inspired by the Lord, He quickly confirmed this plan in a number of supernatural ways. For example, a guest preacher came to the congregation. Without knowing what Ken and I had been talking about and in front of all the people, he looked at us and said, "The Lord shows me there is going to be a big change in both of your lives," and he called on the congregation to pray for us. Only the two of us knew at that time that Ken was planning to step down from eldership to take care of the company, while for me it was the other way round – I was going to dedicate myself to the congregation. We looked at each other; we knew this man was right. And subsequently the entire fellowship unanimously accepted the new arrangements. So at the end of 1992 I stepped down from being Director of Galtronics and on 1 January 1993 I became pastor of the Peniel Fellowship here in Tiberias.

'The geographical location of the fellowship has seen many changes. In 1978 we started as a home group in Tiberias. Then we rented the house I showed you on the way up here, which is where we came under severe persecution towards the end of 1983. At first we felt it right to stay put. But after four weeks of being attacked at every meeting, the Lord put on my heart a sense of urgency to leave that place. I shared it with the brothers and they agreed, and so the next day we removed our few belongings, including our piano. And it was as well we did, because a day or two later somebody broke in and set fire to the place.

'For the next five years we met outdoors. During the first two and a half years of that time, we met at different locations around the Sea of Galilee, gathering at the places where Jesus ministered! Sometimes we met on the shores of the lake; sometimes on one of the hillsides. Then we were a group of approximately sixty people. After that we found a youth hostel just outside Tiberias where we met during the wintertime. Later it became our permanent meeting place.

'Eventually we outgrew that place and moved back to Tiberias into the Galilee Experience (a Messianic bookshop/giftshop), which was comfortable for the adults but not so suitable for the children, who didn't really have enough space there. We were blessed with a large group of children.

'While we were meeting there, "they" [i.e. the orthodox Jews] attempted to set fire to the building. Trying to find a solution to the need for a suitable meeting place for our children, we moved into a local hotel. But it wasn't long before the orthodox managed to apply enough pressure on the owners, and after only six weeks we had to move out of there and back into the Galilee Experience.

'In the year 2000 I felt we had been moving around enough. We had no money to purchase a building. But in faith, one night as I was driving home, I felt urged by the Holy Spirit to drive into this industrial area – this was a street I had never driven through before. As I drove through slowly in the dark, I saw this building for rent or for sale. So we started renting it and then purchased it, and by the time we purchased it, we had all the money we needed. We never took a bank loan. By the time we had to make the payments, we always had the cash to pay. We've outgrown the place now! It holds 300 people and with the lobby here we can seat 330. Our attendance has gone up at times to 370... and if everybody came, we would number 450. So we've grown; we have had nearly forty baptisms this year so far. We preach in Hebrew, but we translate into English, Russian, Spanish and Arabic (for the Sudanese). The Druze speak Arabic but they all know Hebrew.

'The message we preach is always a challenge to draw close to the Lord and be faithful to Him; to be willing to take up the cross and literally die for Him if needed. I see the first challenge, purpose, calling or job that I have before the Lord is to be found faithful on the day of His return. So we are constantly challenged to repent and examine ourselves and to consecrate our lives continually to Him. In this way we become His light and salt in the earth.

'We celebrate all the biblical feasts. Half of them were fulfilled in the first advent of Christ; half of them are prophetic, yet to be fulfilled. It's very interesting to see the meaning of them all – none of which are understood by most in the church. And yes, the feasts are of significance to Christians too. They are significant to anybody who believes in Jesus and has an interest in God's plan of salvation for mankind. The biblical feasts are actually God's "time milestones" in His plan of salvation for mankind.

'As I look ahead to the future, at the moment I see we're in the springtime – a time of growth, new life and expansion; a time when things look promising in the Body of Y'shua in Israel. We have about eighteen home groups in the congregation. And we keep working and seeking to establish new ones. We have many children and young people; I estimate that about 50 per cent of the congregation is under the age of thirty – that's a lot of potential. However, I know from the Word of God that storm-clouds will be gathering at some point. After the spring will come summer – I have no idea whether we are talking ten years from now or less or more; but I do know that Jesus says that before He comes, "When you are persecuted in one place, flee to another. I tell you the truth, you will not finish going through the cities of Israel before the Son of Man comes."[28] So persecution will come sometime, shortly before He returns, when we will have to run from one city to another. At some point God will allow these powers of darkness to erupt like a volcano. And I believe this persecution will come from within – from the orthodox Jews – from within our own country; they will chase us from town to town.

'Today we experience growth and I see that continuing, but already we are being challenged. Already we are in danger. I never announce the exact time or location of baptisms – only the people being baptized know. I never make this public. We are half underground. We are not for exposure. We do not have an internet site. We are very careful what we write. We want to keep a low profile – even towards the Christian world. There are wonderful things happening here. We see many healings. Last *Shabbat* we saw somebody healed of kidney stones. Some time ago, an Arab pastor came here – he was full of cancer – and somehow the Lord laid it on his heart to come here for prayer. Two weeks later I met him and he told me he was healed – the doctors couldn't find any trace of the cancer. As I read the Word of God, I see that Jesus shunned publicity – He said, "Don't tell, don't tell," and the more His fame grew, the more difficult it became for Him. They wanted to crown Him and He had to escape. And so I'm not in favour of publicity, I don't think it does any good.

'My message from Tiberias to the church in the nations is quite simple: Wake up – the time is short and you are not in a good place at all. I speak out of love, not out of criticism. And with regard to Israel, watch out – don't fall into the trap of believing the media and thereby finding yourselves taking the side of the enemy by criticizing God and what He's doing. You have to recognize that what is happening with the State of Israel is God's doing. It's not a historical mistake or an evolutionary development; God's hand is behind it, so you have to get your relationship with Israel in order, both individually and corporately. Start praying for and blessing Israel – that's what the Word of God says – and you will be blessed.

'Pastors have a big responsibility before God to guide their flocks properly and bring correct teaching concerning Israel. They should have nothing to do with Replacement Theology. Pray for us. We are at the cutting edge of God's prophetic will being fulfilled. We are in a battle. We need the backing of the church in the nations. The devil understands what the church has failed to understand. This is why he fights us tooth and nail and is trying to destroy us as a nation and as believers.'

We had talked for a long time. Now it was time to catch the bus back to Netanya. Before leaving, I took a final walk around the building. As I stood in the empty auditorium, I felt this was a place where the pastor and the people are making a spiritual difference in Israel... contending for the soul of the nation... fulfilling Israel's destiny.

CHAPTER 6

Evan Thomas

The bus journey from Tiberias back to Netanya that Monday morning was another fascinating experience. For me, travelling through such well-known places – places we read about in the Bible – is always evocative. So much has happened in the region; so much has yet to happen. I was on an express bus packed with people, both Jews and Arabs, who obviously used these buses every day and knew the area well. I wondered what it would be like living on the slopes of Mount Tabor, or in Nazareth or Cana, or on Mount Carmel, not to mention the Jezreel Valley... How many of them understood the significance of these places?

A couple of hours later we were driving along a dual carriageway and nearing Netanya. I was expecting the driver to pull off the main road and take a slip-road into the town. However, much to my surprise and dismay, he pulled over to the side of the road, stopped by a bus shelter and shouted 'Netanya!' So there I was, on the side of an extremely busy road with no town in sight. I had agreed to call Evan Thomas when I arrived in Netanya, but where was Netanya?!

Feeling very hot and out of place and with my black suitcase on wheels beside me, I was just wondering what to do when a taxi drew up. 'Netanya?' I asked him feebly. And he pointed to a dirt track leading away from the road up an embankment, and then drove off. So, pulling my suitcase behind me, I proceeded to climb up the path and there, at the top of the embankment, I saw Netanya.

Eventually, after several calls on our mobiles, Evan found me sitting on a bench outside a large store on a strategic corner, and we drove to the building where the congregation called Beit Asaph meets – the congregation which Evan co-leads along with David Loden and another elder, Lev Guler.

So who is Evan Thomas? Curiously, he is a Jew from New Zealand. As we will discover, he came to live in Israel in the 1980s – drawn by the same mysterious attraction that drew so many of the other people I was meeting whilst researching this book. Part of the intrigue of his story is how he met the other Jewish believers coming to live in Israel at that time, and how they started to organize themselves and explore their corporate destiny.

Once again I found myself inside what looked from the outside like an industrial factory unit. I noticed there were a lot of women gathered outside. 'Our food and clothing distribution centre is open this afternoon,' Evan explained. Inside were a team of people busily organizing tables covered with clothes for all ages, all neatly arranged according to size. And on other tables I could see food parcels being prepared.

Evan showed me round the building: the youth department; the kindergarten; the rooms where the children met for their classes on *Shabbat*. Everywhere the standard of decoration was impressive. Posters on the wall were handmade and it was obvious they were keen to produce the best teaching aids possible with the resources available.

At the end of the corridor Evan led me into his office. 'Here at Beit Asaph in Netanya we have a co-equal eldership,' he explained. 'So because we are functioning in Hebrew we call ourselves "elders". My work is pastoral, so therefore I'm a pastor. But it's not a title – my title is "elder". I serve alongside two other brothers – one also from an Anglo-Saxon background, David Loden, and the third elder, who has been with us for the past four years, Lev Guler. Lev is a Jewish immigrant from Russia; he came to Israel in 1994, and we have trained and discipled him. He really has a lovely calling on his life and is now serving as a full-time leader in this congregation. He has the advantage of having Russian as his mother tongue, and as 65 per cent of the congregation are from a Russian-speaking background, that is not just an advantage, it's a cultural necessity.

'We are very different personalities with very different backgrounds, but together we provide a strong and stable leadership which, with all the complexities of an Israeli Messianic community, is essential. We have always been an innovative and pioneering entity and I think the variety of gifts we share enhances that.

'The congregation has been in existence since 1978 and we've been in this building since 2000. Over 200 people come here each week, drawn from a mixture of backgrounds – native-born Israelis, immigrants from the former Soviet Union, people from Spanish-speaking South American countries, others from Romania, plus one or two French speakers.

'Because this building is strategically placed within easy reach of the local population, it's been a natural extension of our work to have an "open house" policy to help the needy around us; hence the clothing distribution centre. Local people get to hear about us by word of mouth and they don't hesitate to come here, as you have seen today.

'We have a large group of teenagers in the congregation and many younger children too. As well as having a local programme for the youth, we are also involved at national level. Youth work has a special emphasis because the numbers of young people with a strong faith and an equally strong sense of destiny are growing dramatically in Israel. We train and equip them for the work and many, like Joel Goldberg, are serving with us here. Joel is highly qualified; he grew up in Israel and attended the summer camps run for the children and young people by Messianic believers, so he knows the situation here and the country intimately. He's a dynamic guy and he's established a youth training centre in this building to serve the national Messianic community. Our local teenagers reap the benefit of this because our youth leaders get well trained, and at the same time our kids enjoy a good facility here. So we are the organizational hub for several national summer camps and outreaches. And we're sending some of these young people abroad; this year a team of five were involved in overseas mission work during the summer.'

Evan Thomas was speaking with enthusiasm. Yes, the need in Netanya was challenging this congregation; but looking at Evan, I saw a man with vision and ideas, unfazed by setbacks and seeming impossibilities, especially when it came to the matter of reconciliation between Arab and Jew. As well as his work as an elder at Beit Asaph, Evan has been closely involved with Salim Munayer, an Arab Christian and the founder of Musalaha, the Arabic work for 'reconciliation'. I was interested to hear how Evan discovered he had such a heart for the Palestinians, as well as for his own Jewish people.

'I think it began in 1983, soon after I emigrated here from New Zealand with my wife Maala. From the start I became involved in organizing high-profile evangelism campaigns aimed at the local Jewish population, which met with a lot of indignation from the Jewish orthodox community. We were young and full of zeal, and the orthodox community was not happy about us bringing the name of Y'shua into the heart of Israel and saw us as a rather noisy threat. Quite surprising too, in those early days, was the indignation we received from the international church. Because we were causing quite a stir amongst the Jewish people, this apparently interrupted their Jewish/Christian dialogue programmes. Understandably, we became a source of embarrassment to them. The Jewish population has historically been very hostile to the gospel. The Holocaust continues to happen "yesterday" in the minds of many Jewish people, so it can be very hard for our kinsmen to make a separation between our mission work and what Nazi Germany had done to the Jewish people.

It was during this time that one particular incident greatly influenced my thinking. We had organized a large campaign in Haifa with teams of people operating with military-style precision all over the city. Over a hundred evangelists from congregations across the country came to help us. On the first evening, as we were conducting a training session, there was a knock on the door and a group of ten Arab Christians from the Galilee area walked in, led by Anis Barhoum. "Excuse us," he said, "but we heard the Messianics were holding an evangelistic campaign here in Haifa, and we want to know if we can help you." Among this group with Anis were some Baptist ladies from Acco. It was amazing that here they were, ready to come and work alongside us, and we hadn't even thought about inviting them!

'It was my job in this campaign to co-ordinate the teams and get them into place. I remember taking a van with these Arab Christian Baptist ladies from Acco – who, incidentally, spoke perfect Hebrew – to the beachfront, where there were several thousand Israeli people enjoying the sun. These ladies had bags full of books in Hebrew and I watched as they spread out and moved across the beach in pairs. Immediately they began engaging their Jewish "neighbours" in conversation, speaking about the resurrection of the Messiah – the good news for their people. A few people came to faith during that outreach – all of them as a result of the activity of those ten Arab Christians. Through this experience God really caught my attention and introduced me to the world of the Arab Christian community.

'I was also a combat soldier in the Israeli army during the first *Intifada* in the 1980s, serving in Gaza and the West Bank on some hard tours of duty where again, from time to time, I encountered some of my Arab brothers in Messiah. There was I, an Israeli soldier in uniform, carrying arms against them. This really made me vulnerable to what the Lord was saying, and a huge passion developed in my heart for the Arab Christian community. I was impressed by their zeal.

'During a subsequent outreach in Haifa, about a

year later, we attracted a crowd of about 200 people while preaching in a park. As we spoke about Y'shua this crowd gradually turned into an angry mob, which can happen sometimes, and the situation began to look dangerous. As team leader, I felt it wise for us to retreat slowly, as the mob were beginning to make quite violent advances towards us.

'Unbeknown to me, there was a young Palestinian Christian on the edge of the crowd. He later told me he was from a nominal Christian background and had been moved by what we were saying, so much so that when the situation began to turn ugly, he stood between us and this Jewish mob. He confronted them while we quietly retreated. He stood his ground and calmed them down by speaking to them. Again, my heart was touched by the action of this young Arab Christian.

'When Salim Munayer and I were studying Biblical Counselling together, back in 1988, we became friends and started to talk about the issue of reconciliation. He shared the vision of Musalaha that the Lord had given him. At that stage he was starting to plan ways of bringing young Jewish and Arab believers together, and he asked me if I would like to join him. It took me about three minutes to decide – my heart was ready for such work, and a few months later we set out on our first desert encounter with a bunch of young Israelis and Palestinians, several of whom are now leading congregations.

'The key thing that God taught us right from the beginning was that we were not going to succeed on the basis of bright ideas or dialogue, and certainly not through conferences or seminars regarding our respective theologies about the Land; rather, it would succeed through the building of sincere friendships. The goal of every desert encounter we organized was to build relationships. If we couldn't foster good relationships, there was no hope of being able to sit down at a table to discuss theology. Believe me, like politics, theological issues are taken very seriously here!'

I was interested to press Evan on this issue and asked him if, over the years with his involvement in Musalaha and reconciliation between Arab and Jewish believers, he'd had to compromise his theological beliefs.

'First of all, I am not a dogmatist. I realize that much of my theology and understanding of the social and political situation here is a work in progress. This is partly due to my New Zealand background. I came from a stable family where there was always a lot of dialogue; my father encouraged me to keep an open mind. To give you an example, when I first came to Israel I passionately believed in the Zionist cause; and I have maintained that. While I may have modified my position over the years, nevertheless I've always believed that the formation of the State of Israel was a fulfilment of biblical prophecy. At the same time I see the growth and development of the Messianic community as an even more profound sign of God's Word for the nation and inseparable from the formation of the State. So, I believe Israel has an important place – Jerusalem in particular – as a homeland for the Jewish people.

'However, at the same time I have also learnt not to be so accepting of all that's included in the Christian Zionist package; here I try to make a clear distinction between biblical Zionism and Christian Zionism. So whilst I hold an uncompromising biblical Zionist position, my early Christian Zionist position has modified greatly because I saw the shortcomings of such views – particularly with regard to how exclusive they were regarding the profound work going on within the Palestinian community. I had to have the courage of my convictions, which involved becoming an advocate for my brother on the other side of the checkpoint.

'God taught me so much. I began to love aspects of Palestinian culture and Palestinian worship – their music, their hospitality. I loved their zeal for the lost within their community and their zeal for the finished work of the cross, which I think historically has been quite weak within my own community of faith. What do I mean by that? The Palestinian Christian community emphasize what Y'shua accomplished on the cross. In doing this they provide a strong example for us Jewish believers; by comparison, the Messianic community has emphasized the eschatological aspects of who we are in relation to the Land – that is, God's fulfilment of prophecy regarding Israel, and the resurrection of the Jewish component of the Body of Messiah. Whilst these are important issues, they are not necessarily primary issues. I see within my own Jewish community that Y'shua's victory on the cross has become secondary to theology regarding the Land, so I have actively sought to remedy this in my own local congregation and found very willing partners in David Loden and Lev Guler.

'So when I'm functioning in the context of Musalaha or any forum to do with reconciliation, I go into it knowing that I am going to be in intimate fellowship with people who may actually be strongly opposed to aspects of my theology but yet, hopefully, through the fellowship we share we will be able to build relationships that can develop.'

So what is Evan's motivation for pursuing this reconciliatory work? Does he consider that the Palestinian

113

Arab Christians hold the key to the salvation of Israel?

'When I saw those Baptist Christian Arab ladies on the beach in Haifa sharing the gospel with Jewish people, I realized then that they held a key. That was a revelation to me and caused a paradigm shift in my thinking. It was a big enough challenge for us young Jewish evangelists, with all the hostility we encountered, both with the people we were reaching out to as well as from people we thought would be supportive of us but were not. Some of the leaders of the Messianic community were very nervous about what we were doing because we were being proactive and therefore provocative. So there we were, young and "hot blooded", going out intent on introducing Y'shua [Jesus] to a Jewish society who believed that you could not believe Y'shua was the Messiah and still remain Jewish. At the same time we were suddenly confronted with this other part of the local Body, Arab Christian women, who had a desire equal to our own for reaching the Jewish people.

'A little later, at an international forum in the early 1990s, Salim and I were invited to speak at a large gathering of Campus Crusade for Christ in Basel, Switzerland. We had no idea what we were going to. When we stepped up to the podium we found ourselves in front of an audience of 11,000 people! We simply told our stories – the Palestinian Christian and the Messianic Jew – stories that reflected our deep friendship. Much to our surprise, this was a life-changing encounter for many. So when we talk about "keys", whilst one key is in the hands of the Palestinian Arab Christians witnessing to Jewish people, there is another key that is perhaps even more powerful, and that is when people see us functioning and fellowshipping together rather than separately. And of course, we shouldn't be surprised at this, because it is a basic truth that when those in the world see us, Arab and Jew, united because of our belief in Y'shua, then they are drawn to Him, the One who makes this possible.'

Evan had earlier mentioned the growing numbers of Jewish young people becoming believers who are radical in what they believe and who are not afraid to talk about Y'shua to their friends. What sort of impact are they going to make here in the Land as well as outside of Israel in the future?

'I think the impact is going to be enormous. My greatest passion and the thing I invest most of my time in is training young people. For those who are clearly leaders – we train them to be better leaders. We channel their zeal for reaching out to the lost by training them in evangelism and leading missions.'

What is their understanding of their destiny, both within Israel and beyond, as young Israeli believers, in the light of biblical prophecy and the times in which we live?

'They believe this is the season they are to be proactive in mission work. So next year [2008] we are planning to take a graduate class from Israel College of the Bible to Goa in India to reach young Israelis there. Lech L'cha is a short-term discipleship programme that has been functioning for the past few years. They frequently take teams out on summer missions to places like Uganda. Lech L'cha are the words of the Lord to Abraham – "go forth".[1] They train young Israelis for mission exclusively among non-Jewish populations. Many local congregations, including our own, are sending teams out on mission to different parts of the world. This summer we sent a team to southern Ukraine. Generally we evangelize to the Jew first, but inevitably this spreads out to the general population. So yes, we feel the call to be a light to the nations. This is something we talk much about. Increasingly we want to see finances and human resources going out from Israel and helping communities that are less well off than we are, providing teachers, evangelists and so forth – and it's starting to happen, especially when we send out teams comprised of both Jewish and Arab believers. When people see us genuinely functioning and expressing fervour for the Messiah and love for each other, it's really something very special. All that's needed is for them to share their testimonies and the Holy Spirit does the rest.

'If I look at the past twenty-five years and see what's happened, it's hard to believe – Y'shua and His community of followers are once again on the map nationally; ministries are being developed and are proving to be fruitful. In the Western mindset it might seem insignificant, but when I see our young people being trained in evangelism, and answering God's call to go out on missions, that's exciting. When I see established Messianic congregations planting new communities throughout the Land and setting them free to develop their own identities, it's remarkable. Israel's destiny is to once again fulfil its ancient calling to be "a light to the nations". As pioneers, my generation of Messianic leaders laid the foundations. Now, as we see the young people, "the Joshua generation", emerge and take responsibility, we know that God's purposes are being fulfilled. Israel's hope and the hope of the nations is being revealed!

"Blessed are You, O Lord our God, King of the universe, who has given us life, established us, and brought us to such a time as this!"'

CHAPTER 7

Arie Bar David

It was Tuesday morning and I was in Jerusalem. I'd taken a bus from Netanya late the previous night spending a delightful evening with Evan Thomas, his wife Maala and their daughter Sara. Hotels can be lonely places when travelling alone, so it's a real treat to be invited into a home; it speaks of acceptance, and I love it!

Now I was staying in Ramat Rachel, a *kibbutz* hotel on the outskirts of Jerusalem overlooking Bethlehem. Many tour groups stay at this hotel – it's welcoming and the food is delicious. There is a regular bus service from Ramat Rachel into Jerusalem, so after an early breakfast (and breakfast in an Israeli hotel is a feast!) I was on my way to meet Arie Bar David at Yad Hashmona, a *kibbutz* run by Messianic Jewish believers near Abu Gosh, a village off the main road halfway between Jerusalem and Tel Aviv.

'Jump in a Sherout taxi to Beit Shemesh,' Arie told me, 'or bus number 185, and get out one stop before Newe Ilan at the Elvis Presley roundabout.' I'd been to Yad Hashmona some years ago and remembered seeing the larger-than-life statue of Elvis set incongruously in a small service station just off the main road.

The bus drove off and I began to walk up the long

steep drive to Yad Hashmona. It was mid morning and the temperature was rising fast. The rocky ground was parched. Tall grasses, dried by the summer heat, had turned almost white. I passed pomegranate trees laden with ripe fruit. And sparrows could be heard chirping in their characteristic way – a familiar sound in Jerusalem. Reaching the reception building, I stopped to look at the view – I was in the heart of the Judean hills. Nothing had changed here. As far as the eye could see the hills rolled on. Rocky outcrops glistened white against tall, slender conifers that scattered the hillsides. In spring, after the rains, this would all be green and a sea of wild flowers. Today, in the heat, everything shimmered and was still. It was peaceful and beautiful.

It was too soon to see Arie, so I found a shady spot and was just enjoying a cold drink when a group of Australians came by. Apparently they were on a course being run at Yad Hashmona. It was their first visit to Israel and they had come to work on a project connected with a Messianic group based in the Tel Aviv area and were spending a couple of days on a training programme. Listening to their enthusiastic conversation, I was struck yet again by the number of groups coming to Israel from the farthest corners of the world, at great expense to themselves on what must be the trip of a lifetime.

It was time to find Arie Bar David. I had been told he was somebody with vision; a person who understood Israel's destiny. Why had he decided to come and live on this Messianic *kibbutz* in the middle of the countryside, and why had he started a biblical guiding centre?

I began to walk back down the drive towards Arie's house. Yad Hashmona is a collection of buildings – a mixture of homes and communal areas. Arie and his family are 'members' of the *kibbutz* which was founded by a Finnish group of Christians in 1971. When the Finns arrived, there were no buildings, just a bare hillside. By 1974 they had built some houses, and several years later Arie came here with two of his brothers; they were youth leaders at the time, running a summer camp for young Messianic Jews. 'We were in the Parachute Regiment,' he told me in his heavy Israeli accent, 'so it was like a military camp with lots of Bible studies!'

Arie's story is unusual. His early life and his experience of being a child in Israel during the early years of Israel's independence after 1948 have shaped him and given him a passion for his country. But perhaps the biggest factor in moulding his thinking and belief was the fact that his parents were Messianic Jews; as far as they knew, they were the only Messianic Jewish family living in Jerusalem in 1948.

Arie told me he was born in Jerusalem in the Hadassah Hospital on Mount Scopus in 1947. 'My father travelled from Bulgaria to Israel in 1928. He came from a prosperous and intellectual family and later studied at the University of Zurich, Switzerland. He told us how, as a young student, he didn't believe in God – Bulgarian Jews tended to be very atheistic – yet he was intrigued to discover whether God really existed. So he studied philosophy and astronomy in an attempt to find God, and economics in order to help his father with his business. It was in Zurich that he eventually met the Lord. He'd been there for many years and after completing his doctorate he described feeling a sense of emptiness and despair, because despite all his studying, he hadn't found what he was really looking for.

'One day he was sitting in his room when he heard

music in the street outside his house, so he went out to see what was happening. A group of musicians were playing brass instruments – trumpets, trombones and cornets –and he liked the sound they were making. As they passed along the street, one of the people with the musicians took a pamphlet from his pocket and handed it to my father; it was a copy of the Sermon on the Mount found in Matthew's Gospel, chapters 5, 6 and 7. He didn't realize it then, but these musicians were members of the Salvation Army. Returning to his room, he read the pamphlet and as he read those words spoken by Jesus, it gradually dawned on him that this was what he had been looking for.

'My father was a very intelligent man. He spoke eight languages fluently and was well read. He particularly liked Tolstoy. He believed that when you read a book it should be in the original language, not a translation. His search for the meaning of life had lasted many years, but as he finished reading those chapters from Matthew, he knew he had found the answer. The next minute he found himself talking to God: "If this is the truth, I'm going to leave everything I've been doing and I'm going to tell my Jewish people about the Messiah." He had never heard of the Holy Spirit, but he later described how he felt the presence of the Holy Spirit at that time. He was crying for joy! For three days he didn't leave his room. His friends thought he had lost his sanity. When he eventually went back to the university it was to return all his books – he told his tutors he had found what he was looking for!

'However, his parents did not share their son's enthusiasm when, on returning home, he told them about his "discovery". Rather, they were appalled to hear of their son's new-found faith in Y'shua. This was impossible for them to accept and, like the families of many other Messianic Jewish believers who have trodden a similar path, they were angry, hurt and grieved over their son. He had turned his back on his own Jewish people by believing in the God of the Gentiles – Jesus. For a few years they did not want to see him and he was banished from the family home and cut off from any inheritance.

'But despite being rejected by his family and finding himself alone in the world, my father remained convinced that he had found the truth. After considering his options and realizing he had no future in either Europe or Bulgaria, aged twenty-three and single, he came to Palestine, as it was then. Being fluent in many languages, he soon found work as a translator and also worked on the land in the orchards. However, finding work and the wherewithal to support himself was simply the prelude; his real desire was to find a group of like-minded people with whom he could study the Bible. After searching Israel, he found a Bible College in Bethlehem and for three years was the only Jew in a class of Arab students! By this time he had met and married my mother,' Arie continued. 'She is still alive and I love to talk with her about those early days. They were pioneers in every sense of the word. They were proud to be Jewish and proud to be living in Israel. At the same time they realized they were two of only a handful of Messianic Jewish believers living in the land; in fact, to begin with, they were entirely alone – they didn't know of any other believers.'

And so, the environment Arie and his brothers were born into was challenging; it was to get rapidly more dangerous.

'My father regularly taught us children the Bible, with only a Hebrew Bible – he didn't believe in using commentaries,' Arie told me. 'In those days we knew we were the only Jewish Messianic family living in Jerusalem. When the War of Independence started in 1948 my father decided not to leave Jerusalem even though we were living in an Arab area and it was dangerous. And it wasn't long before Jewish families living in our area were being attacked by local Arabs – in fact several families were killed before the British soldiers eventually arrived on the scene to protect us. They came just in time to rescue my father, who was attacked and seriously injured by a group of Arabs. It was obvious we had to move to a safer part of Jerusalem and the British soldiers brought us to a house in Prophet Street, where we lived throughout the remainder of the war. As a family we studied the Bible together four times a week and every night we got down on our knees and prayed together, even when it was very cold in the winter. I therefore grew up understanding that Israel was the land given to us by God and as Jewish believers we had to be in the land; we were inseparable.

'In 1955 my parents decided it was time to leave Jerusalem because life had become impossibly difficult; we were ostracized and hated by our Jewish neighbours because we were Messianic believers. So we moved to Haifa and it was paradise! As a family we continued to gather together every evening to pray and sing; my mother and brothers were all very good musicians. I remember that on one of our first evenings in Haifa, the neighbours knocked on our door to ask if they could come in because they enjoyed listening to our singing! We were amazed because in Jerusalem, whenever we sang hymns the neighbours would yell at us to stop. Much later on I realized that some of our Jewish neighbours were Holocaust survivors and many were mentally sick.

They didn't open their shutters. They never went out. Captive to their memories and the voices in their heads, they couldn't hear any music.

'I now realize what a unique childhood I had. We studied the Bible in Hebrew and I remember, as a child, reading in Isaiah 6, "Be ever hearing, but never understanding; be ever seeing, but never perceiving."[1] As I looked at the people living around us, I saw that we were surrounded by deaf and blind people. We were able to understand from the Scriptures exactly what was happening around us; we were living it! And so I knew that what my father was teaching us was right; I knew we had the "light". There was never a time in my life when I doubted God and I always believed that my destiny was linked to that of Israel.

'In 1964, when I was seventeen years old, I first started to become aware of other believers. I remember it well because I was at a Messianic "youth" camp. There were forty people there aged from four to eighty-four – we were the only Messianic Jewish believers in Israel at that time! Looking back now, I consider it such a privilege that I was in that group. We all knew each other – it was like one big family. In fact today many of us are interrelated through marriage.

'During the war of 1967, when Jerusalem was re-captured from the Jordanians, I was in the Parachute Regiment and we fought some hard battles. One month after the war had ended, Yitzhak Rabin, the then Chief of Staff, gathered all the paratroopers (at that time there was one brigade) to Augusta Victoria, to the little theatre on the Mount of Olives, and there he gave a speech. For me this was very significant because I knew I had been born in the building I could see behind him, but for nineteen years it had been impossible for any Jew to go there because the entire area east of Jerusalem had been in Jordanian hands. And here I was, some years later, looking at the place where I was born, this time as a paratrooper. This made a lasting impression on me. I was just nineteen years old but on that day I understood the prophetic significance of this event. I understood that God had helped us to win back Jerusalem; we couldn't have done it on our own.

'In 1973, during the Day of Atonement War, I found myself fighting alongside Ariel Sharon in the Sinai against Egypt over the Suez Canal. We fought a fierce battle during which I saw an angel of God. I understood from that experience that we only won that war because God was with us. However, when I listened to the speeches of some of our politicians praising the brilliance of the Israeli army in defeating the Egyptians, I felt they weren't giving due honour to God; in their eyes the army had replaced our need for God, and this disturbed me.

'Before joining the army I was a member of the Israeli Young People's Philharmonic Orchestra. After the Six Day War in 1967 the actor and singer Danny Kaye (who was Jewish) came to Israel and arranged to take our orchestra on a world tour to show that Israelis were not just good fighters but were also good musicians! So for four months, in the middle of my army service, I found myself playing in concert halls in all the major capitals of the world. We were a big orchestra of almost 100 players. And we were a good orchestra; the famous violinist Itzak Perlman was one of our soloists. Danny Kaye was our conductor on this tour and I spent many hours talking with him; I don't know why but he liked me! There were twelve other soldiers in the orchestra and Danny Kaye loved to hear about our experiences fighting in the war. As it happened, I was the one who had seen the most action, so he singled me out and asked me many questions. So I was able to talk to him about Jesus and my faith, and I told him that as far as I could see, it was a miracle that Israel had won the recent Six Day War against Egypt. I told him how on one occasion, along with two other soldiers, I had captured a group of 200 Egyptian soldiers! They were so frightened. Whatever we told them to do, they did immediately! It was a miracle. However, every time we moved on to another capital city in Europe and the stories were told, all the honour was given to the victorious Israeli army. I hated it. And I hated it when people wanted to meet me because I was a paratrooper. I told Danny Kaye that I wanted no part of this. Very few people in those days dared to give honour to God and to be humble. Most of the army people liked all this adulation. They didn't have spiritual understanding about these things or the humility to accept that it was God who gave us the victory.

'When I finished my army service I was immediately offered a job with the Jerusalem Symphony Orchestra as a full-time musician playing the double bass. It happened one Friday. I had just finished my duty. I was hitch-hiking home. I was in uniform. It was raining and then, at last, somebody driving a Ford Escort stopped his car and called out, "Arie, get in!"

'It was the conductor and manager of the JSO. He said, "What are you doing?"

'I replied, "You can see what I'm doing!"

'Then he told me that he needed me in the orchestra urgently because two days earlier one of the double bass players had suffered a stroke and died. Now I hadn't played my double bass for a year because I had been in the army. This encounter seemed more than a coincidence because I knew that usually you had to wait years to win a place in this orchestra. So I went home and took my double bass out of its case and started to play!

'Two weeks later I attended auditions to find there were at least ten other double bass players competing for this one position and some of them were very good – but he chose me! So I found myself in the orchestra and I played with them for the next seven years, and at the same time I was put in charge of security arrangements for the orchestra when it travelled abroad. (After the Munich Olympic Games, when several Israeli athletes were murdered, every group of Israelis travelling abroad, such as an orchestra, had to have somebody in charge of security.) I had to plan ahead and carry a pistol at all times. I had to keep one eye on the conductor and one eye on the audience to make sure nobody tried to attack us. It wasn't easy.

'I remember we were touring England in 1976, performing in several cities from the north to the south. During one of the concerts we had a call to say the IRA had planted a bomb in the building where we were playing and we had to evacuate the premises immediately. There was a coffee shop nearby, so the entire orchestra went there and we started to play Hasidic music and the people loved it! The bomb alert turned out to be a hoax and everybody went back into the concert hall. Greatly encouraged by the enthusiastic response of the audience in the coffee shop, we played with added energy. It was one of the most enjoyable concerts of the tour. The audience had so enjoyed the concert in the café that they were keen to hear more and gave us rapturous applause.

'I was young to have a permanent position in the orchestra. But, after seven years, I knew it was time to move on. For me, Y'shua was more important and I sensed I was going to be doing something entirely different. When I handed in my resignation people were shocked and wanted to know why I was turning my back on such a promising musical career. After my final concert with them they held a farewell party and I told them how much the past seven years had meant to me, but now I needed to pursue my own destiny – and that meant leaving the orchestra. They knew I was a believer in Y'shua – over the years I had shared my faith with everybody in the orchestra. And so I went to the Hebrew University for two years to continue my musical studies in the Rubin Academy; at the same time I was preparing to move on in whatever way God showed me.'

Meanwhile, in 1970, Arie married Esther. In July 1981 they moved, with their three young daughters, to Yad Hashmona (by now a Messianic *kibbutz*). Arie's two brothers and one sister had also decided to live at Yad Hashmona. He told me the conditions for joining the *kibbutz* were to sell your property and give all you had to the community.

'Since these were the rules, we accepted it as God's will for us. We sold our apartment in Ramat Gan and gave that to Yad Hashmona, as did others. It was a "second chapter of Acts attitude" in an Israeli *kibbutz*. When I came here I was asked to run the carpentry workshop. To begin with I had no idea how to go about things. But gradually I began to learn the necessary skills and today the furniture we make here is sold all over Israel. It gradually became a profitable business and we ended up employing twenty people. At the same time, once a week, I taught music in a conservatory and prepared many students for their examinations. I specialized in teaching harmony and improvization. I loved it!

'But as the years passed, I sensed God was taking me into yet another area of work, and in 1992 I started to study to become a tour guide, and four years ago it became my full-time job. For a while I was running the carpentry shop, teaching music and fitting in a little guiding, but I was trying to do too much. It soon reached the point where I realized that I wanted to spend more time guiding groups, but I wasn't sure how it was all going to work out. Around this time I was with a group of pastors in the mountains of Sinai; it was a mixed group of Arabs and Jews. Without my asking, they asked if they could pray for me. David Loden and Evan Thomas were part of this group. Historically they knew me for my carpentry; I made the furniture they have in their houses. But on this occasion, they told me how God had shown them that it was time for me to move out of the carpentry work and start guiding full time.

'And that's what happened. Now I combine my knowledge of the country with my knowledge of the Bible. It's as though all my life has been a preparation for this time. My father taught me how to study the Scriptures in Hebrew. My time in the army has taken me all over the land. My tours involve intensive teaching and much hiking. Sometimes we spend one week in the mountains of Sinai, when I share the meaning of God's name. At Ein Gedi we look at the life of David and Jonathan; I want to teach Christian tourists the importance of studying the Old Testament stories and the prophets. I was a commander in the paratroopers, so I teach about leadership. And I teach about how to survive in the desert as well. Many of my groups consist of people who are going to be missionaries – people who will have to face tough conditions.

'Today I understand that what I am doing is linked with Israel's destiny. When we were young my father told us that we would live to see 70, then 700, then 7,000 believers here in Israel! He was right. As a tour guide I want to teach people the importance of understanding what Israel is in the eyes of God. I find many people are ignorant about so much in the Bible. To me the Bible is like a map; we have to navigate every little detail – every word is important. And so I try to give understanding about the physical birth of Israel and the link between the land and her people.

'Today the religious Jews realize our numbers are growing. More and more Israelis want to know about Y'shua. Now I am keen to take groups of young people and teach them the Bible in Hebrew, just like my father taught us. It concerns me that so many Bible teachers only use English translations of the Bible. There is a new openness amongst our youth in Israel; they are frustrated and they are searching. I want to show them Y'shua as our Jewish Messiah; so often they think of him as belonging and connected to the Vatican and the Catholics, and as a result they believe Christianity is Catholic. Many of our Jewish poets wrote about how the Jews were persecuted by the church – and for years this is what our young people read. This material was taught and studied and caused entire generations of young people to feel so disgusted with Christianity that they wanted nothing to do with Jesus. However, as time has passed and modern historians have come to the fore who do not just write with a historical perspective, the minds of Jewish people have been opened and today we have a new generation. We can sense the openness when we talk to them. They are not brainwashed like my generation was.

'Given this new freedom of thought and openness to hear about Y'shua, I believe my role is to show our young people the land of the Bible. I believe in this way we are influencing and changing the minds of people as to who Y'shua is. Being a guide is the perfect medium for sharing in this way. The Israelis are just the same as any other nation – memories are short. Now God is having to apply pressure – look at the war with Lebanon. He is bringing this nation back to Himself. When I read the prophets and look to the future, I see we have hard times ahead with hard wars to fight – and as one who has fought in four wars in the front line, I know war is a time God can use to get people's attention. Every second Israeli realizes we have trouble ahead.

'As well as guiding groups of young people, I am keen to train more young Messianic believers to be guides themselves. So I have started a Biblical Guiding Centre here at Yad Hashmona to teach believers who are already licensed Israeli tour guides more about the Bible and how they can teach their groups, whether they are Jewish, Messianic or Christian, the relationship between the Bible, the land of Israel, the believers who live here, the church and the nations.'

Walking back down the drive to the bus stop, I thought about Arie's story. The memories of the child being taught the Scriptures by his father; fleeing from the Arab mobs in 1948; the anger of their Jewish neighbours when they sang hymns together as a family; his disdain of the attitude of many in Israel who, rather than recognize the hand of God in helping them to win so many wars, gave the honour to the army; and now his desire to pass on all his experience to the younger generation as he sees a new freedom in the spirit of the nation and a curiosity as to who Y'shua is. Arie is a man who, even as a child, linked his destiny to Israel's, and who has always put this calling first.

CHAPTER 8

Howard Bass

Arie Bar David's story was unusual; born in what was then 'Palestine', his entire life had been lived in the context of a Messianic Jewish family. Now I was on my way back to Jerusalem for an early evening meeting with somebody who would tell a very different story.

The bus journey would take an hour or so, traffic permitting. By now it was late afternoon and my next appointment was at 6.15 p.m. at the Dan Panorama Hotel with Howard Bass, a Messianic pastor from Beer Sheva. He was in Jerusalem for a meeting later that evening and had one hour free beforehand; this was a window of opportunity I did not want to miss.

I arrived at the Dan Panorama on time, only to find the hotel foyer was full of people. I had never met Howard before and had no idea what he looked like, so I decided to call him on his mobile phone. 'I'm just parking the car,' came the reply. 'I'll be at the hotel entrance in a couple of minutes.'

As we didn't have long, we ordered a coffee from the bar and managed to find a relatively quiet corner. Clipping the mikes onto our lapels, I pressed 'record' on my mini-disc and so began our conversation.

'Who are you?' I asked.

Howard told me how he and his wife Randi came to Israel from the United States in September 1981 and moved to Beer Sheva four months later in 1982, 'Because,' he said, 'that's where we believed the Lord wanted us to be.'

'But why did you come?' I asked him.

'Because of Jesus! We came here seven months after getting saved! I'd been here twice as an unbelieving Jew, once as a tourist and once as a volunteer on a *kibbutz*, and although Israel was important to me, it didn't feel like "home". However, Jesus made Israel home. We didn't know anybody or have any relatives here. My wife is not Jewish. We were married less than a year and a half before we came to Israel, but now we have four children who were all born here. One has finished the army, two are in the army, and one is in the tenth grade at school.'

We had covered quite a lot of ground in a very short time. I was interested to find out how Howard had been so sure that his destiny was linked so closely to Israel.

'It took thirty-one years for God to save me, but when it happened it was very quick and very radical, and everything changed in a moment. To start with, I was not the man my wife married, which frightened her a bit. And secondly, I believed that Jesus would be coming back very soon.'

'And you knew immediately that you had to come to Israel?' I asked.

'Well, I distinctly heard the Holy Spirit telling me to go to Israel. Now that made it home. Before that, I didn't want to leave America and come and live here. But once I heard God telling me to come, I couldn't wait to get here! It didn't matter what I thought about it before. However, although I was sure, I wasn't so sure my wife would share my enthusiasm about leaving America. So I prayed, "I assume you mean both of us," meaning my wife and I, "but you need to tell her!" And that was probably the best prayer request I've ever made.

'Just after we got married we'd been on a cycling tour around the US looking for a place to live. Then when we got saved and were just starting our "new" lives, it seemed right for us to go to Israel. So, seven months later, we came as tourists with our bicycles. We were put in touch with David and Lisa Loden by someone in Arizona who owned an apartment in Netanya, where they live. So when we got off the plane we moved into that apartment. When we first met David and Lisa I didn't tell them we were going to live here because Randi didn't know that yet. But once we did know we were meant to live here they said, "We've heard that before!"

'We based ourselves in Netanya and from there travelled around the country finding out where the believers were living. This was Randi's first visit to Israel, giving her an opportunity to see the country, and before long we both felt the Lord was leading us to Beer Sheva. We'd lived in Arizona for five months and I think that prepared me to live in the desert. Prior to that we were from Virginia which enjoys four seasons every year. After a month of travel Randi reached her own conclusion that it was God's will that we should live here and that we should obey Him. So I was really happy that He answered that prayer, and we changed our status from tourists to new immigrants.'

I was interested to know whether Howard came from a religious family.

'I grew up as a conservative Jew and Randi grew up in a conservative church. She left the church when she went to university, and I left the synagogue after the Six Day War when I was seventeen. God used that war to help me identify with my people so that I became a Jew first and then an American. However, at the same time I left the synagogue, the time came to celebrate the High Holidays [September onwards]. I told my parents that I wasn't going to the synagogue that year. They were concerned. But I argued that it was hypocritical to only go to the synagogue twice a year – we were no better than the Christians who only went to church at Christmas and Easter. I told my parents that if I had sinned against them, I was sorry. At that time I didn't know whether there was a God; but I also hoped there was. And because I identified myself as a Jew, I never looked for answers in any other religion. I was a Jew and believed that if there was a God, then He created the heavens and the earth, He was the God of Abraham, Isaac and Jacob, and He was the God who chose us to be His people. At that time I certainly didn't believe in Jesus, because then I wouldn't have been Jewish! I wasn't attracted to Buddhism or Hinduism because they didn't believe in this one God – so I couldn't be a Jew and believe that. Gradually I got involved in liberal politics; that was the Jewish "religion" in America when I was growing up.'

'When you felt convicted to come to Israel, what was your vision? What were you going to come and do?' I asked.

'I didn't know! I'd just been born again and at the same time I heard God telling me to go to Israel. We didn't know anybody here. We came to Israel without any backing – we just came because God told me to come.'

'What happened when you first went to Beer Sheva?'

'We got to know some believers as we travelled around the country and they put us in touch with a couple of families here. We also visited the Bible House Bookstore in downtown Beer Sheva and that's where we met a Finnish believer; he was the first employee of the bookstore, which was owned by the Christian and Missionary Alliance [an American church]. They also owned a property which is where our congregation now meets. So whilst we've had a long-term working relationship, we are not a CMA church, but we work together in Beer Sheva. We've been very blessed to have these properties to make use of. And so, back in February 1982, we joined a group of about twenty other believers and we officially became immigrants and started learning some Hebrew. I had learnt some in America in the synagogue for Bar Mitzvah purposes, but Randi spoke no Hebrew when we came here. And so we started to settle down.

'However, at the same time, a couple belonging to the Lubavich movement – an orthodox Jewish religious group who are very anti missionary activists – came to Beer Sheva from Richmond, Virginia, the city where I grew up. They knew my former best friend and they came to the same absorption centre in Beer Sheva where new immigrants were being taught Hebrew and, knowing that we were believers in Y'shua, they started harassing us and speaking against us to others, with the result that nobody would speak with us and we weren't able to continue with our language studies. Instead we met with the Goldbergs, another Messianic couple living here, and they helped us with our Hebrew.

'So we met with opposition early on – but God used that experience to prove that He is with us and for us. He did bring us here and He is keeping us here. All those who turned against us actually left within a year and went back to North America, except for the Lubavich couple who moved to Tiberias, and caused some trouble there, before moving north to Safed – and as far as I know they are still there, writing their anti-gospel, anti-Christian, anti-Jesus books.

'A year later, in February 1983, I got a job working for an engineering company as a clerk. It came about because one of the believers in our congregation was an engineer and he invited me to come for an interview at his company, although I am not an engineer by background. The first time I applied, they didn't interview me. However, I was invited to go in again and this time the director – who, because I have a degree, saw I was overqualified for the position on offer – asked me whether I was desperate for a job! I replied I wasn't desperate but yes, I would like to work. He said he could take me on immediately, but what would happen if I found something better the next week? But I told him that if he offered me a job today, that would be my job and I would not look for another. So he took a chance and hired me and paid me a little bit more than he needed to because of my qualifications, and I stayed with them for six years until they closed down their offices in the south in Beer Sheva. Then another company called me to ask if I would work for them in a similar capacity. So I worked there for the next eleven years, until I became the full-time pastor of the congregation in 2000.

'I had been the treasurer of the congregation, then a deacon, and then one of three elders – I never thought I would become the pastor. For two and a half years we prayed for a pastor. We'd grown to the point where we had three elders and we were all agreed that none of us were meant to be the pastor. So we continued to pray, and during this time an increasing number of people were telling me that I was the one who should become the pastor. Then others from outside the congregation, who were objective, started talking to me about it. Finally, after two years, I asked the other elders if I was meant to be the pastor. And they were both glad. At that point I accepted that the Lord was pointing at me and I couldn't get away from it. The final confirmation came when I was invited to give my testimony at a Russian-speaking service, which was part of our congregation. At the end of the meeting somebody stood up and said, "Why are you disobeying God?" For me, this sealed it and although I didn't feel entirely comfortable about becoming the pastor, in the end I had no doubt that God was telling me that this was what He wanted.'

I was watching the time and wanted to bring Howard's story up to date as well as talk to him about the future and Israel's destiny. 'We're now in 2007 – what has kept you busy?' I asked.

'Trying to get the congregation to know who we are in Christ. We are living in a society that rejects us. Some people who are getting born again were born here and are having to leave the security of their former "society" to join us. Others are immigrants coming into the country, mostly from the former Soviet Union, which is where 42 per cent of the population of Beer Sheva originates from, and in this group the unemployment figures are high and there is a lot of hardship.

'And by the way, I talk about Jesus, Christ, Messiah, and Y'shua... to me they are all the same person; I believe it's important for Israelis to know Jesus is the same person as Y'shua.'

That was refreshing to hear! I asked Howard to tell me about the young people.

'I believe God is going to use our children not only to turn the hearts of the fathers to the children, but also to turn the hearts of the children to their fathers, because they are growing up in a country that is rebellious. As I see it, Israel is a country in rebellion. It always has been. It's in the Bible for all to read. It hasn't changed. And this rebelliousness is also evident in the church throughout the nations as well as in the congregations here in Israel. And of course, this shouldn't surprise us, because the Scriptures tell us that in these last days there is going to be a lot of rebellion.

'As for our young people, some are zealous for their faith, and some aren't. Some are born again yet they are caught up with earning a big income and the wrong sort of music. I spend a lot of time with our young people because I believe they are in danger of being too focused on themselves and are therefore missing the bigger picture. Indeed, here in Beer Sheva, we are self-absorbed – we don't get many people visiting us from abroad. But God is going to change it. My hope is in Him. And He does have a time schedule. We don't know the exact day or hour, but we should be aware of the times in which we live.'

'How do you see the relationship between what is going on here in Israel and what God is doing in the church in the nations?' I asked.

'Well, the Bible says that until the fullness of the Gentiles comes in, Israel remains partially blinded. I think we will see a lot more Gentiles getting saved before we see more Israelis being saved. I think we will see a lot of Muslims getting saved before we see more Jews being saved. And God will use the Gentiles, especially the Muslims; He will give them a new heart and a new spirit and they will

139

start provoking Israel to jealousy and will start showing mercy to them instead of wanting vengeance. And these same people will provoke many Arab Christians, many of whom don't see Israel's significance because they don't want to see it at this point – it's too close to them. But when they see all these Muslims coming in who have had a revelation, who have been delivered, God is going to use them to wake up the church among the Arab nations.

'In the near future I am expecting to see breakthroughs into the Bedouin community and also amongst the Sudanese refugees who are coming here. They can speak Arabic, so I believe God will use them.'

And with that our meeting was over.

A few weeks later I was back in Israel with a group of Christians from the UK. Remembering what Howard had said about few people visiting Beer Sheva, we went down there! We drove from Jerusalem via Hebron. Gradually the landscape changed from sparse vegetation to desert and majestic sand dunes, their silhouettes clear against the cloudless blue sky. Occasionally we passed an oasis where date palms loomed tall. We passed Bedouin encampments complete with camels. We saw shepherds leading their flocks of sheep and goats across this arid landscape and wondered what they were finding to eat. Our guide told us that the ground was covered in nutritious seeds from the grass and flowers that grow in the desert in abundance after the winter rains which turn the desert green in springtime. It seemed as though biblical sights were around every corner.

After a couple of hours we saw Beer Sheva in the distance – a large sprawling industrial town built on a plain, bearing testament to the way in which Israel has managed to develop cities even in the desert. As we got closer, we passed apartment blocks and hotels, offices and shops. A modern city. Driving through, we reached downtown Beer Sheva and eventually pulled up outside the Bible Bookstore (Ha-MaKoM) that was making no attempt to disguise itself.

'Yes, we're often attacked by the religious Jews here,' Howard later told the group. 'In nearby Arad they're having it much worse than us, though.'

The bookshop incorporates a coffee shop, and as we sipped drinks, Howard told the group the story of his congregation. Then we walked around the corner and through a shopping district to the building where the congregation meets, and there we met Howard's wife, Randi. We walked through the house into a large courtyard covered by a makeshift roof made from corrugated aluminium. 'We need that to shade us from the sun in the summer and from the rain in the winter,' Randi laughed. 'We meet outside here every Saturday – there are too many people to fit into the house these days.'

Howard said, 'It's our battle to not only hold onto the ground which is ours but also to resist the moves of the false "winds" – also translated "spirits" – to snuff out our light which is to glorify our heavenly Father and Messiah Jesus our Lord. The challenge within the Body remains to build it up with love and the truth, and letting the Holy Spirit have His place to sort through much of what hinders in our lives and others' lives.

'God has called Israel to be a light to the Gentiles [i.e. non-Israelis/Jews], both as a nation and also as individuals who understand their part in the whole. Israel is fulfilling this destiny now only in part, and generally speaking, without intent. The Scriptures given to Israel have been printed and distributed throughout the world and its nations. The Messiah Himself, coming as a Jewish Israeli, is *the* Light who has come through His people to the Gentiles; the Lord's apostles, including Paul, were Israeli Jews through whose word and teachings many Gentiles – and Jews too – have believed in Jesus.

'Israel, whether in good standing with God or poor, is, by the Word of God, "a light to the nations". She is a visible demonstration of the sovereignty and faithfulness of God to His Word and covenants for those who will "see the light". Israel and the Jewish people are His witnesses of a holy and righteous Father God who knows how to train up those who would be His children, family, people – and mature to being sons and daughters who know and take an active, positive interest in their Father's business.

'Since God has given Israel as an example to the church – made up of both Jews and primarily Gentiles – then Israel is a light to Christians for what it is to be a "nation" chosen by the Creator and Redeemer and under His direct authority. Most of the times in which the apostles use Israel as an object lesson to believers, it is *not* to be like them! Rather, we are called to learn from their experiences with God and appreciate the need of all of us for God's mercy, and to appreciate our need for His salvation by grace.

'The millennial Kingdom to come will see Israel fulfil her call to be "a light to the nations", and for her to realize that this call was to be a blessing for the nations, to draw them to acknowledge and worship the one true God, and so receive all His benefits.'

We left Beer Sheva that day, having touched on one of the 'outposts' of God's work in Israel. Jerusalem may be 'denominational headquarters', but here we witnessed a relatively small group of people not only surviving in the midst of opposition and persecution but also growing in number. Their desire to reach out to their Muslim neighbours – whether Bedouin or Palestinian – is uppermost in their minds because they understand what a strategic people they are in God's plan regarding Israel's destiny.

CHAPTER 9

Arthur Goldberg

How is it that Israel is going to be a 'light to the nations'? This was the question I was seeking the answer to as I travelled around Israel in September 2007. What evidence is there today that this tiny nation can and will affect the nations of the world as described in the Bible?

It was Wednesday, 5 September. I was off to meet Arthur and Zellah Goldberg. They live in Modi'in, which meant getting a bus from Ramat Rachel into Jerusalem and a Sherout taxi to Modi'in. And the journey into Jerusalem took ages! Half an hour stretched to two hours. Something had happened in King George Street and the traffic was at a standstill. Eventually I reached the central bus station and found the right Sherout. There were two other passengers – a religious Jew and a secular Jew. I mentioned in a previous chapter how important identity is in Israel, and identity is usually determined by what you wear.

The driver asked me what I was doing in Jerusalem. 'Working,' I replied; it is always my policy not to volunteer too much information early on.

Not prepared to take one-word answers, he pressed me further: 'What do you do?'

'I'm a writer.'

'Do you live here?'

'No.'

'Where do you live?'

'England.'

And at that his eyes lit up. 'Then I will play you Princess Diana's favourite song!'

Feeling uncomfortable about being the focus of attention, I wondered what song would come out of the CD player. It was 'Lady in Red' by Chris de Burgh. How bizarre! The religious passenger continued reading his prayer book, the other fellow looked bemused, and I was amused!

The journey took a couple of hours; I got off the Sherout in the town centre. Modi'in is an attractive new town. The streets are wide and tree lined. It's quiet and the housing, a mixture of apartments and houses, has been carefully planned. I called Arthur and within a few minutes a car pulled up. It was Zellah. A couple of minutes later I was inside their modern apartment. Photographs of their family were everywhere. And on one wall hangs a large collection of china plates – souvenirs from around the world from a lifetime spent travelling, Arthur explained.

Arthur's father was Jewish, although his mother was not.

'I was born in Baltimore in 1940. During my early years I was very aware of my Jewishness. I went to Hebrew school when I was six years old until my Bar Mitzvah at the age of thirteen. I wanted to become a pilot, but because I had paralysis in my right eye I was not able to do this, so instead I went to university and studied Aeronautical Engineering. However, in less than a year, I left to join the US Navy so I could go on an aircraft carrier and work on aeroplanes.

'After I had been in the Navy for a couple of years, I was stationed in San Diego, California. One of the men in my unit was a Christian and he was after me! I told him to leave me alone because I was Jewish and not interested in Jesus. But he was very persuasive and kept asking me to go to meetings with him. I tried to put him off by telling him dirty jokes! But one night I was sitting in the base and didn't have anywhere to go, so, reluctantly, I went with him to this meeting. They were singing and shouting and clapping; I thought they were "holy rollers"! But the girls were great and I was a young sailor, so I kept going to these meetings just to be with the girls. And they were really nice to me. My future wife was one of those girls!

'One night my Christian friend left a Bible with me whilst I was on guard duty. I started reading and that very night – I remember it vividly – I gave my heart to Y'shua. When I read, "It would have been better for them not to have known the way of righteousness, than to have known it and then to turn their backs on the sacred command that was passed on to them",[1] the Holy Spirit convicted me.

'Two days later I was involved in an accident and spent several weeks in hospital, where I read the Bible right through and the New Testament three times. I fell in love with God's Word.

'We married in 1961 when Zellah was eighteen and I was just twenty – we were very young! We decided to go to Moody Bible Institute in Chicago, believing we were destined to be missionaries in Brazil.

'Still hoping to become a pilot, I enrolled onto the Missionary Aviation course at Moody and had just completed the first month when I met the director walking in the hallway. He said, "Mr Goldberg, why are you wearing glasses?" I explained that my right eye had been damaged when I was born. He then told me that he was very sorry, but I could not obtain a licence for commercial flying in any country wearing glasses – I had to have 20:20 vision in both eyes. In that instant my world crashed around me.'

Zellah continued, 'Now I'm not Jewish, I'm from Chicago, and I grew up in a little church that focused on Israel. I had many Jewish friends. My mother loved Jews, for some reason. The fact that I married a Jew seemed irrelevant at the time, but it was a nice benefit. My heart was always with the Jews. I had no desire to go to Brazil! But I didn't know how to tell my husband and I'd been praying for weeks, "Lord, either you have to change me or him!"'

'That evening,' Arthur carried on, 'I was sat in our local Jewish community centre in Chicago, where I helped out; it was run by Messianic Jews. And an elderly woman, a Messianic Jew from Poland – a very obnoxious person! – called me into her office: "Goldberg, get in here! Tell me somethin' – are you blind? You don't see nothin'! The Lord is talkin' to you. You don't hear nothin'! You don't see nothin'!"'

'I was trying to understand what this old lady was talking about. She went on: "First of all, you come and you're the leader of the Jewish Prayer Band, you live in a Jewish neighbourhood, you work in a Jewish workplace – what's the matter with you? What are you doing going to Brazil? You're blind. You don't hear nothin'!" And all of a sudden I understood.'

By now Arthur and Zellah were both weeping. These

events had happened forty years ago, but it could have been yesterday.

'I got home. Zellah knew nothing of what had happened that day; we didn't have mobile phones in those days – we didn't even have a phone at home. I walked in and she said, "Before I make dinner, sit down, because I have to talk to you."'

They were both weeping again.

'So I sat down, and she said, "I can't go on like this. I have to tell you I have a greater love for these [Jewish] people in Albany Park than I could ever have for native Indians in Brazil. I love the Jewish people."

'We both realized what was happening. We fell on our knees and wept before the Lord and committed our lives to our people. One of the professors at Moody Bible Institute was a man called Nathan Stone. He had been director of the Jewish Missions programme at the institute for many years. The next morning, after all of this trauma, I went to school early and found him in his office. I asked if he could talk to me for a few minutes. He was a Jewish man from London and a wonderful believer. I told him what had happened the day before and how I felt I needed to change to the Jewish Missions course (called the Jewish Studies course today). And he started crying. He wept like a baby. I was looking at him, not understanding what was going on. All I'd done was ask to change my course! So I asked him what was wrong.

'When he was able to collect himself, he said, "Goldberg, a year and a half ago, when your application came into school, they immediately advised me that we had a request from an Arthur Goldberg, and I started praying for you. I knew that you were applying for the Missionary Aviation course, but I prayed and asked the Lord to give you a love for your people. And today it happened!"

'We stayed at the Moody Bible Institute for another three years and graduated in June 1966. By July 1966, just one month later, we had moved to Israel and I enrolled at the Hebrew University to study Archaeology and Semitic Languages. To support the family, I taught at the Anglican School in Jerusalem. In the meantime we had another baby, our third boy, and the Six Day War happened.

'We stayed until 1969 and went back to the States for two years, where we had our fourth son. I went to an Aviation School in New Mexico and became officially licensed as an aircraft mechanic. We came back to Israel in June 1971 as new immigrants with Israeli citizenship and four little children. We lived in Lod, close to Tel Aviv, and I was hired in December 1971 by Trans World Airlines as a mechanic and spent the next thirty years there.

'In those early days not only were there very few believers in Israel, but there were very few activities for believers. In 1969 I was one of the founding members of the Messianic Assembly congregation along with people like Victor Smadja; we even had an Arab elder. The MA was the only Hebrew-speaking congregation in Jerusalem at that time. Zellah and I became involved in the summer camp programme, and it was there we met young people like Daniel Yahav and Arie Bar David.'

At this point Zellah produced an old photograph – a picture from one of the early youth camps. Arthur said, 'We soon realized we were raising the next generation – the generation who are the leaders of today. The whole purpose of the camp programme was to win the children from the believing homes and bring them to a personal saving knowledge of Y'shua. Today, forty years on, we have expanded to between 10,000 and 15,000 believers.'

'When did you start being interested in the Christian Arab community?' I asked.

'I had come from an American culture and had grown up in a home where there was no prejudice,' replied Arthur. 'I did not have any hang-ups about Arab brothers and sisters in Israel. Now it's imperative to understand that the early youth programmes and family programmes and children's programmes made no distinction between Arabs and Jews. In fact, at family conferences we would have a Hebrew speaker with an Arabic translator and an English translator, or an Arabic speaker with Hebrew and English translators. We were all in close fellowship together. One of my dearest friends was an Arab brother from Nazareth. He and his family would come and spend a weekend with us; and likewise we would go to Nazareth and I would speak in their church.

'Things started to change during the mid to late 1970s. I was very busy working and was often outside the country for long periods of time. The children grew, and by the 1980s our eldest son went into the army, closely followed by our second son. In 1982 Israel was at war with Lebanon; both of our sons were in that war.

'Then in late 1982 a conference was organized in Greece under the auspices of African Enterprise with Michael Cassidy. This was to be a conference of reconciliation. We were there with other Israeli Messianic leaders, alongside Christian leaders from places such as Syria, Lebanon, Algeria and Iran. That conference was one of the most significant experiences of my life. We cried as we met one another.

'After I spoke, one of the brothers came up to me and

he said, "Brother Goldberg, I'd like to give you something."
He was from Lebanon and he was a Palestinian. "I'd like
to give you something that I have never given to anyone
else and that you have never received from anyone." And
he put his arms around me and hugged me. And he said,
"You have just received a hug from a Palestinian who
hated the Jewish people and hated Israel, and it's the first
time I've expressed love to a Jewish person." We cried. It
helped me to realize that he was a brother.

'But something even more significant happened
when we came down to breakfast the next morning. A
pastor from Aleppo [in Syria] was there with his son of
twenty-five. It was a small dining room and we sat at a
table and this pastor's son was sitting opposite me. He
looked up and started crying. I said, "Are you OK?" And
he said, "I have never met a Jew in my life, and I can't
believe that you are here and that you are a Jew who loves
the same Jesus that I love." We both were crying.

'Looking back and looking at what is happening
today, despite the troubled political situation, we believe
that we had a part in building the foundation for what
is now spreading from Israel into the rest of the world.
Increasingly, Jewish and Arab believers are having an
international impact by their unity – the unity that comes
from the faith they share in the death and resurrection of
Jesus. The Scriptures that mean so much to us are those
that talk of the "one new man":

> For he himself is our peace, who has made
> the two one and has destroyed the barrier,
> the dividing wall of hostility, by abolishing
> in his flesh the law with its commandments
> and regulations. His purpose was to create

> in himself one new man out of the two,
> thus making peace, and in this one body
> to reconcile both of them to God through
> the cross, by which he put to death their
> hostility.[2]

'Israel's destiny is to be a catalyst for the world, to show that reconciliation is possible and can be achieved. Jewish and Arab believers in Israel will set an example for believers worldwide, exemplifying that living out love and unity in Y'shua is a tangible reality.'

And with that we shared lunch together. Humus and olives! Then it was time to get on the bus back to Jerusalem.

I had been talking to a couple who have been instrumental in building up the body of believers in Israel over the past forty years. They have seen the numbers of both Arab and Jewish believers increase so rapidly since the 1970s that today there are more believers in Jesus in Israel than ever before. Talking to them reminded me that the most surprising things going on in Israel today are happening in the spiritual realm, out of most people's sight. From AD 70 until 1948, Israel as a nation state did not exist. The Jewish people were dispersed throughout the world. However, slowly, as if drawn by some invisible magnet, a hundred years ago Jewish people started to return from the nations where they were living to 'Palestine', as it was then called. Israel is now a thriving nation with major highways, a modern airport, and modern cities full of people. Today the Jewish population worldwide is approximately 13.3 million. In 2001, 8.3 million Jews lived in the Diaspora and 4.9 million lived in Israel. I find it interesting that considering their relatively small numbers, the Jewish people and the nation of Israel remain the focus of world attention. The question is 'Why?' What is Israel's destiny?

CHAPTER 10

Eitan Shishkoff

I was due to meet Eitan Shishkoff back at Ramat Rachel at 4 p.m. Although living in the north of the country, he was in Jerusalem for a couple of days – another fortuitous opportunity which I was keen not to miss. Thankfully, the earlier traffic chaos in Jerusalem had sorted itself out, and I got back from Modi'in just in time.

So who is Eitan Shishkoff and why is his story relevant to Israel's destiny? He told me he was sixty years old and a grandfather. But this gentle description belies a colourful history because Eitan, like others whose stories are told in this book, used to be a hippie in America. His Jewish parents had 'spared no expense to provide the best', he told me, but 'like so many disillusioned college-aged youth, I dropped out of university. Three months and 3,000 miles later, I found myself in Central Park, New York City on 15 April 1967 with 100,000 anti-war protesters. There my draft card fell victim to a match. I burnt it in defiance of the US government.'

After a disillusioning attempt to begin a new life in Canada, far from the US role in Vietnam, he returned to California. In 1969 he married Connie (also Jewish) and moved to New Mexico where they attempted to 'create a truly free alternative. Our first home was a cave. Encountering rattlesnakes, lack of rain, disease, personality conflicts, and bemused locals, the next four years were spent learning to survive. Wood-burning stoves, outdoor toilets, kerosene lanterns and hauling water in buckets became a way of life. Connie almost died twice of child-bearing complications. Our commune broke up. Reading Hopi and Pueblo Indian mythology, studying astrology and the *I Ching* and attempting Eastern mysticism, we were searching hard for a spiritual understanding of life.'

In 1972 one of Eitan's closest friends was murdered. Where was his soul? This question dogged Eitan's thoughts. The answer came through a meeting with two 'Jesus People' who told Eitan about Y'shua and showed him that Israel's rebirth as a nation had been foretold in the Bible. By 1973 others in their group began to discover Y'shua. 'People's lives were being transformed before our eyes, becoming fuller and more peaceful than they ever thought possible,' he added.

Eventually they left the remote mountains and came to a Bible school/outreach centre called Shalom, in Santa Fe, New Mexico. In 1975 they met a Messianic Jew named Eliezer Urbach who had survived the Holocaust. He began teaching them about how to live a Jewish life as followers of Israel's Messiah.

Longing to be part of a Messianic congregation, Eitan and Connie ultimately found themselves in Washington, DC, where they joined a congregation called Beth Messiah and helped develop a growing community of both Jewish and Gentile followers of Y'shua.

In 1989 Eitan had a vision in which he saw an oasis with tents full of provisions of every description. 'It was a heavy download,' he told me. 'I was stunned.'

At this time Eitan had for years been dreaming of returning to Israel. He had just started working amongst America's newly arrived Russian Jews. Eitan had studied Russian during the 1960s when he was a 'pagan' and in 1989 God instructed him to pick up the language again.

'When you learn somebody's language you're saying that you're prepared to sound foolish in order to communicate with them,' he told me. 'So one thing led to another, and for several years we worked amongst Russian Jews and saw many coming to faith, which was encouraging because we'd been witnessing to American Jewish people for years with little effect. These Russian Jews, however, were spiritually hungry; in fact they embraced our message.'

Increasingly Eitan's thoughts were occupied by the desire to live in Israel and to help pioneer the Messianic movement there. In November 1992 he and his family made the move. I wanted to know how Eitan was so sure it was right to come to Israel.

He said, 'Fifteen years earlier, in 1977, I attended a conference in Kansas City on "The Holy Spirit and Evangelism" and heard a talk given by Shira Sorko-Ram. She spoke about the calling Messianic Jews have to return to the land of Israel and be a part of seeing Israel return to the Messiah. While she was talking the Holy Spirit spoke to me and said, "This is your destiny. I intend for you to live in Israel." It was so clearly from God that I never doubted it and from that time on I expected it to happen. Twelve years after this experience, by then fully involved in serving a Messianic synagogue, I had the oasis vision. It was 1989. That marked the beginning of our intensive work with Russian Jews in America.

'Whilst I kept the vision of the oasis and tents of mercy to myself, I did talk about making *aliyah* [moving to Israel] with my colleagues in the States – especially Asher Intrater, who was destined to arrive in Israel in 1992, the same year we arrived. We visited Israel in 1987 and I saw how young the Messianic movement was. I made several more trips after 1987, and with each trip, there was further confirmation as I made contact with Israeli believers. I met Claude Ezagouri, Daniel Yahav and Eric Morey on that first trip. They were very accepting and encouraged us by saying there was a place for us here. When we arrived and I started language studies, almost every other student was from the Soviet Union. Then I understood clearly what God had been doing. Because of the time of preparation in the States, responding to His leading to study Russian and leading a small Russian-speaking ministry, I was able to make contact with some Russian-speaking believers in Haifa.

'At first we joined a new congregation on Mount Carmel led by David and Karen Davis and Peter and Rita Tsukahira. A couple of years after we arrived, a small prayer conference was held – there were less than twenty people. David and Peter asked me to speak about what I believed God wanted to do amongst the Russian-speaking immigrants. This would help them to know how to pray. The Lord led me to the passage in Jeremiah[1] where God says that He will bring back the captives and restore their tents with mercy. I was stunned when I read that chapter, because those were the very words God had whispered to me in 1989 when I saw the tents of mercy in an oasis; until then I had never put the two together! As I shared that night, it was the first time I had spoken about the vision in public, and immediately people began to pray in earnest for a work to be birthed specifically among the Russian Jewish people in the Haifa Bay area. Ten months later, in December 1995, Tents of Mercy started.

'During those ten months, God clearly directed me to the book of Acts, and I realized this was the blueprint for how we were to operate – through living as a community of believers sharing our lives with those around us. I believe that God's design is to live in community, serving and helping each other, while reaching out to serve the society we're a part of. We began by organizing home cell groups. We discovered who the needy were in our locality and began to distribute aid to these people. News soon spread and in 1997 we met with opposition [from religious Jews]. This opposition became violent when the small warehouse we gathered in was firebombed in the middle of the night. It was a defining moment; a test to see if we would run or stay. We stayed. And now, twelve years later, we have a network of five congregations and a couple of warehouses. We also run a soup kitchen, a pro-life counselling service and an outreach to women in prostitution.

'I have a passion to see all Israel saved. We desperately need a spiritual revival that will bring our people back to the purity and power of the God of Abraham, Isaac and Jacob. Two thousand years ago a radical movement of Jews embracing Y'shua as Israel's promised Messiah began in Jerusalem and spread, eventually around the world. However, today He has become a foreigner in His own house, and faith in Him is considered by most to be un-Jewish.

'How can that be changed? How can Israel rediscover the very One who can transform our nation? This is a question I ask myself daily. Of course, there is no one answer. But after living as an Israeli and praying for God's light of revival to shine upon His ancient covenant people, I have come to at least one conclusion: Israel will be changed through its youth. There are several active, dedicated ministries reaching out to young Messianic believers in Israel today. This is essential. If we only establish congregations and focus on adults, we will not see "all Israel saved". One simple reason for this is that many Messianic Jews in Israel have come from other countries. For these, Hebrew is not their native language. Our children, however, are growing up as Israelis. They instinctively know the forms of communication and relationship. They go to Israeli schools, serve in the Israeli army and are an integral part of the society. Their refreshing testimonies are already drawing Israeli youth to Y'shua.

'I see a new generation of Israeli Messianic leaders emerging before my eyes. These young people have the potential of bringing to Israeli society the desperately needed end-time revival spoken of by the prophets. Joseph, David and Daniel were young men in ancient Israel who found a role that shaped the history of God's people. The disciples of Y'shua were young men too. They changed the world forever. Only when today's young Messianic Jews of Israel are aflame with love for the Lord, equipped with God's Word and emboldened to make Him known in Israeli society, will the prophesied spiritual revival take place.

'The motto of our national youth ministry, HaKatzir [The Harvest: www.HaKatzir.com], is "To equip Messianic youth in Israel to be the workers and leaders in the final harvest in Israel." Yet this and the entire question of Israel's destiny are not only in the hands of Messianic Jews. The prophet Isaiah foresaw a day in which "The Gentiles will come to your light, and kings to the brightness of your rising...[2] The sons of foreigners will build your walls...[3] Strangers will stand and feed your flocks."[4] These statements point to a partnership between Gentile and Jewish lovers of God, for the sake of Israel's salvation. There remains a glorious era of full participation in the miracle of Israel's spiritual restoration. We exist as a physical nation. The first stage of Ezekiel's "dry bones" vision has occurred. But the second stage has only begun. Now is the time for the wind to blow. Wind and Spirit are the same word in Hebrew – *ruach*. Now is the time for us to intercede together for the wind of God's Spirit to blow across Israel, raising the spiritually dead to new life in Y'shua.

'All New Covenant disciples are priests in the house of the Lord. Joel says: "Let the priests, who minister to the Lord, weep between the porch and the altar; let them say 'Spare your people, O Lord.'"[5] This is our shared priesthood, the calling of Jews and Gentiles who love the Messiah. Only together will we see the nation of Israel revived in order to say, "Blessed is He who comes in the name of the Lord."[6] Only then will we see our magnificent King coming in the clouds to take up His throne and at last bring Heaven's reign to earth.'

CHAPTER 11

Zvi Randelman

I had been invited to have lunch with Zvi Randelman at Beit HaY'shua, his drug and alcohol rehabilitation centre in Jerusalem. I am deeply interested in work of this kind; anything that snatches people from the jaws of death and self-destruction and restores them back to life as they were meant to live it is, to me, nothing short of a miracle. In this case I was to visit a newly founded centre that helps both Jews and Arabs under the same roof. Zvi not only pastors a new congregation called Y'shuat Yisrael (which means Salvation of Israel); he is also the founder and director of Beit HaY'shua.

As arranged, Zvi picked me up from Ramat Rachel at 1 p.m., and we drove to the Talpiot district of Jerusalem, a busy industrial zone. After dropping his car off at a place where it could be washed, we walked around the corner and into the building where Beit HaY'shua is situated. We walked up two flights of concrete steps and stopped outside a plain door on a long corridor. Zvi unlocked the door and we stepped into an apartment where I was introduced to the former drug addicts who were on the first stage of their rehabilitation programme. I say 'former drug addicts' because, as I was to hear, this is a centre where drug addicts see their habit of addiction broken amazingly quickly, and within a very short time they are rebuilding their shattered lives.

Lunch was ready and I was shown into the diningroom – a simple, plain room housing a large table, with a piece of gym equipment in one corner. It was a very hot day and the windows were all wide open. Since this was a busy district, the noise from the traffic was deafening.

There were nine of us around that table and of the six former drug addicts, two were Arabs and four were Jewish. Some spoke a little English in addition to their first language – Hebrew, Arabic or Russian. One by one, I listened to their stories of years spent in prison; years spent taking heroin; all from broken families. However, all were off drugs and were looking forward to a future. And all were now believers in Y'shua and filled with the Holy Spirit.

After lunch I sat down with Zvi and started to record his story.

'I was brought up in New Jersey in a traditional Jewish family with loving parents, two sisters and a brother. I remember going to our conservative synagogue on many a *Shabbat*, but it was very dry for me. Nevertheless, I believed in God and would often pray to Him when I had a problem. At age thirteen I had my Bar Mizvah, after which I stopped observing the Jewish traditions.

'Yet, I was hungry to know the answers as to why I existed and what the purpose of life was. I began to search for answers through other religions and philosophies. I began experimenting with drugs. Starting with marijuana, I graduated to heavier drugs such as speed and LSD. In my search I moved through yoga and meditation to *I Ching* and various other blends of Eastern religions.

I found that LSD especially opened me to the spiritual world and I began to take more and more "trips".

'Although I was attending a top-ranked prep school in New Jersey, I lost all motivation for studies. I became rebellious against my parents and society as a whole and joined the hippie movement. These were the years of the Vietnam War, and I became very anti-war. Music also became extremely important to me and I attended countless rock concerts and festivals such as Woodstock.

'Sometimes I felt I was getting close to "the answer", as I called it, but I never actually arrived there. After some really bad LSD trips and other negative incidents, I became disillusioned with drugs and the hippie movement. After the Woodstock Festival, the Altamont Concert in California took place, where a man was stabbed to death by Hell's Angels. That concert really marked the beginning of the end for the hippies. I began to realize some of the hypocrisy in the movement; yes, we were a movement of love, but we really mostly loved ourselves and a few people who were close to us. We didn't understand the real meaning of love. I felt that maybe the answer was to get "back to the earth" – join a commune.

'After finishing high school, I wanted to take a cross-country trip in a Volkswagen van with a friend and then join a commune. However, education was very important to my father and he persuaded me that I should at least try a year at university. So I began studies at the University of Wisconsin, Madison campus – a campus well known for being radical. I remember getting there and seeing the windows of the Physics building still blown out from the Weatherman blast [an organization that advocated using militant actions in their anti-war protests]. Before long I was back to taking acid [LSD] almost every other day with

163

my girlfriend in my search for spiritual reality.

'During the semester break in the middle of a very cold winter, somebody invited my girlfriend and I for a meal at his house one evening. We agreed and we set out. I remembered their family name and the street, but I could not remember the number of the house. So we started knocking on doors. But no one knew this couple and it was so cold.

'Finally we knocked on the door of a brightly lit house – they didn't know the people we were looking for but they invited us in to get warm. The door shut behind us and, much to our surprise, we found ourselves in a house full of "Jesus People"! And they didn't waste one minute – as soon as we entered they started to tell us about Jesus: that He is the way, the truth and the life.

'I didn't know anything about this Jesus. I'd read a little of the Bible. In fact sometimes on my LSD trips I'd read the Bible to see if there was some deep spiritual truth there, especially the book of Ecclesiastes. However, I didn't really understand it. But now these people were telling me that I could have a new life through Jesus and that God loved me. My response was, "Well, whenever I'm high I love everybody."

'I left there angry and went back home. But that night the Holy Spirit started speaking to my heart; I just sensed those people had something I didn't have. I was hungry to know the truth. So the very next morning I took my girlfriend and we went back to that house and this time I was willing to listen.

'I sat on a couch with her and one of the young men (who was also from a hippie background) opened up the Gospel of John and began to read to me, "Whoever believes in me has eternal life", and I remember thinking how good it sounded that I could have a new life and a relationship with God and find real meaning to life – but on the other hand, it sounded too simple. Just believing in Him – how could that be? It's hard for me to explain what happened next – I didn't pray but suddenly God gave me a revelation. Suddenly I knew – I knew that Y'shua was the answer! And as I came to that revelation, the Holy Spirit came on me and baptized me with the love of God. It was a tremendous experience of God's love; a love that is far beyond any human love. I turned to my girlfriend and said, "It's true, it's true." And she accepted the Lord too. I left a new person and I remember praying on the way home, "Lord, take away the desire for drugs."

'I went back home where I had bags full of marijuana and LSD – I was dealing drugs to support my habit – and I threw them all down the toilet. That happened in January 1971 and I've never had a desire for drugs since then. Three days later God delivered me from cigarettes. I also took all the books I had on the occult and Eastern religions and went to a used bookstore and traded them all in for different translations of the Bible in English. Now I would have burned those books – but nobody told me to do that – all I knew was, I had to get rid of them. I began to read the Bible and I could not put it down. I was being led by the Holy Spirit.

'Three or four months after I had that experience of the Lord, I began to read in Ezekiel and Jeremiah about God's plan for Israel, that in the last days God would re-gather the Jewish people from all the nations to which they had been scattered, bring them back to the land of Israel and here He would give us a new heart and put His Spirit in us. And I knew that included me! I then became part of a community of believers in Illinois living on a farm and stayed there for about three and a half years.

'During that time I experienced difficulties in my relationship with my parents because of my faith. When I first met the Lord I had called my parents. I told them, "I've found the answer: it's Jesus!"

'Their initial response was, "Well, that's nice!" I used to share with my Dad about my searching, without mentioning drugs, and I think he just believed it was one of the fads I was going through. But then a few months later, when I kept my faith in Jesus, and especially when I dropped out of university, that was too much for them, and we became estranged.

'In 1974 I felt that it was God's time for me to move to Israel. I'd left university because I'd only begun studies there to please my father – but now I decided to resume my studies at the Hebrew University in Jerusalem. When I decided to come to Israel my father was very happy! I remember travelling to Chicago to meet him, and we met in a restaurant.

'I said, "Dad, what would you say if I told you I wanted to go back to university? Would it matter where I study?"

'And he said, "I don't care if you study in Timbuktu so long as you go back to university!"

"So how about the Hebrew University in Jerusalem?"

'And he said, "That would be wonderful!"

'And that began to repair the damage; in fact he actually paid for the studies. The first year was a *Michena*, a preparatory year where I learned Hebrew. Then I began studies in Biology and eventually did a second degree in Biochemistry and then started a PhD.

'Eventually I established and managed a biomedical

business specializing in the supply of immunologicals, chemicals and diagnostic kits to laboratories.

'When I first arrived here in Israel I didn't know anybody. It was a real step of faith. My room-mate was the son of a reformed rabbi from Chicago. I gradually started to meet some of the believers in Jerusalem; at that time their numbers were small.

'I knew why I was here. I believed that God was restoring Israel both physically and spiritually and that He was going to bring the Israeli people to know Messiah Y'shua. I could see that it wasn't all that easy but that we were in a process and this process would take time. I also began to understand that only the Holy Spirit could remove the veil from the Jewish people's eyes. I've never doubted that God will do it because He says He'll do it.

'It's been a long haul. I've been here for thirty-three years, and I have to say Israelis are much more open today than they were in 1974. We're seeing many more Israelis saved. We're seeing many more congregations starting. We've also seen many Jews come to Israel from the north. We prayed into that for years and then in the late eighties God began to bring a wave of *aliyah* [Jewish people] from the former Soviet Union. We had a million new *olim* [immigrants] come in, and from those people in particular we've seen openness to the gospel.'

'So has your motivation always been to see the salvation of Israel?' I asked Zvi.

'Always. A Jewish person coming back to the land is wonderful. But if he doesn't accept his Messiah he cannot enter into a full relationship with the God of Israel and cannot receive the eternal life which God promises through faith in Y'shua the Messiah. These are the crucial issues of life.'

167

Zvi's wife, Yaffa, is also a Jewish believer. She's from New Jersey, where he was born. She came to Israel in 1976 because she'd been depressed and wanted to get married. She began to study in Netanya at a Hebrew *Ulpan* where she met a Dutch lady who was a believer. They became very good friends and over a period of time, this lady talked to Yaffa about Y'shua and her need for a Saviour. She gave her a New Testament which Yaffa hid under a pile of books because she was so embarrassed about it in the beginning. But she reached a place of desperation where she began to read the New Testament and, much to her astonishment, she discovered that all the early disciples were Jewish! That was a revelation for her. Finally, one day in the bathtub she prayed, 'Jesus, if you're the truth, I'm willing to give you a chance.'

'And that was all it took,' Zvi added. 'She was born again, and we met about three or four months later, and within six weeks we were engaged, and we got married in October 1977. We are the proud parents of five boys, one of whom is married with two children.'

'How did you come to be running a drug rehab centre?' I asked.

'I started a Messianic congregation in 1980 called Succat David,' said Zvi. 'After ten years I felt we were stagnating and we weren't fulfilling what I felt was my call of reaching the Jewish people with the gospel. It was a nice congregation but we weren't seeing many people find salvation and there was little discipleship. I had reached a personal crisis, and in my discouragement I decided to take some time off. I didn't stop serving in the congregation, but in my frustration I actually returned to studying again, this time for a PhD in Molecular Biology.

'After a year of studies I felt the Lord say to me,

"That's enough; I've given you a break but now I've something else for you." So I obeyed and left the university and began to pray, "Lord, whatever you want." I asked Him about the future of the congregation, and He said, "Outreach – that is the future."

'Here in Jerusalem it's very hard to evangelize and see people come to the Lord. And God showed me that there needed to be some kind of centre where people could be soaked in the gospel. I asked, "What kind of centre?" Then the Lord began to speak to my heart about the drug addicts and the alcoholics, and I became really burdened for these people. Now this was something I had never thought of doing in the past. I had read certain books like *The Cross and the Switchblade* and *Run Baby Run* [the autobiography of Nicky Cruz] and had always felt challenged by them. However, I never imagined that I would minister to drug addicts and alcoholics.'

'Is that because you thought you'd left drugs behind many years ago?' I asked.

'No, I just didn't think that was for me. However, after I heard this call from the Lord, my wife and I began to pray about it, and after four months of prayer, I realized I had to take a step. I talked to David and Karen Davis who established a rehabilitation centre in Haifa. Later I called Eric Benson, the director of the Beit Ha Nitzachon (House of Victory) centre in Haifa, and asked if I could come up for a week. I asked him to expose me to the most difficult conditions; I wanted to live with the guys and be there to serve and to learn. He agreed and after a week I was like a fish in water! I knew this was for me. That week proved to me that God would give me the grace to do this kind of work. I continued to travel to Haifa once a week for the next eight months to further my training as well as to build a close relationship with the brothers there.

'After my initial week in Haifa, I shared the vision with other pastors and leaders in Jerusalem, since I believed I had to have the Body of Messiah behind me in this endeavour. They were all very positive and they supported me in prayer.

'For the next year I tried to get things off the ground. I talked to people; tried to find suitable premises; tried to find staff. But by the end of that year very little money had come in – we had about $10,000 and I knew that wouldn't be enough to get started and I didn't have any staff. So I was getting pretty discouraged.

'By July 2004, I became ill with a gastric problem which was very painful. But I sensed that God was in it and He wanted to get my attention, so I began to go in the yard behind our house every night and pray. And God spoke to me and said, "Don't pray about the project; don't pray about your ministry or congregation, you need to just seek me." And so I did.

'It was hard to start with but after a while I began to break through and God showed me areas of my life I needed to adjust; I needed to repent. I would spend hours face down on the grass. Other times I would walk around. God was really doing a deep work in my life. I wasn't concerned about the project any more. I just wanted to break through with Him.

'After three weeks, the verse from John which says, "Without me you can do nothing" became a reality to me. I realized I was totally dependent on the Lord, and without Him I could not even love Him or His Word, let alone serve Him. I was totally helpless. And then the Lord restored me! He gave a prophetic word to my wife and then to me and said, "I've brought you to the time of breakthrough; things are going to go so fast now, you're going to have to run to keep up with me." The illness went away – I was healed. But more importantly, I had new faith, God's faith, that this work was of God and that He was responsible for it.

'Within one month God gave us the place, and brought the team together. I just watched it happen – it was supernatural. For example, in my search for the right staff, I felt led to call a pastor who had a Russian-speaking congregation. We met and as we talked I asked him whether he had any congregational members who could potentially serve as staff in the rehab centre. He said, "No, but I do have a place here for rent." And this is the place where we are currently located. This is it!

'Then somebody told me about Yevgeny, an ex-heroin addict from the Ukraine who had a burden to work with drug addicts. He even had previous experience working in drug rehab. So we met and we hit it off and I sensed God had brought us together. And then Roni joined us; it all happened within a month after a year of struggle. I had no problem believing for finances then. After that experience with God, I knew this was not Zvi's work, this was not man's work – this was God and it was born of the Holy Spirit. But I had to be broken before I could really know that. And when it happened, I was really at peace. I said, "Lord, this is your work, so it's your responsibility to give us the money!"

'By faith we opened Beit HaY'shua. We had enough money in the bank to run for two months and since then – it's amazing! – three years later, we have the same sum of money in the bank today that we had three years ago. The money just comes in every month. We're not well publicized. We don't run fund-raising

171

campaigns. It's a walk of faith. I've been through many financial struggles in my life, but this time, God gave me the faith to believe the finances would come in for this project. God is a supernatural God, so if we trust Him, He will provide. And we found that because we're dependent on Him for finances, we're also dependent on Him for everything else. So when someone is sick, we pray and expect the Lord to heal. We have seen many manifestations of the healing power of God here. Our best efforts will never make it with the drug addicts and alcoholics that God is bringing here; they need the supernatural power of God.

'We interview every new person and they have to bring medical tests to show whether they are HIV positive or have hepatitis B or C; we also ask for a chest X-ray. Then we interview them to see if they are really serious. We also have a two-page contract with the rules of the place; there's a lot of love here but it's tough love. We don't allow smoking. We don't allow walkmans, videos or anything of the world here. They have to obey all the rules of the staff. They have to come to all the meetings. Any misbehaviour, such as lying or physical violence, means they will be kicked out. They also know the programme is faith based – we don't hide that. We tell them we believe the only answer for them is to meet the Messiah, Y'shua. And we tell them that if they give their lives to God, He is able to release them 100 per cent. Recently Sergei came here; he'd been a drug addict for three years. He immediately met with the other guys and joined in with the prayer times and Bible studies and worship times. He wasn't that open in the beginning; he didn't understand too much. Finally, after about four or five days (which for us is a long time), he asked Y'shua to come into his heart, and we've seen the change already. He's reading the Bible continually.

'When a new man enters the programme we don't waste any time. As soon as they arrive we search them. If we agree to receive them we conduct a thorough search of their person and their luggage. We also pray over them that the Lord will help them and heal them of the withdrawal symptoms – and I would say 90 per cent of the time God heals them almost totally of the withdrawal symptoms. They may have insomnia or a few cramps, but these are always very slight – and I think God does that to show He loves them and He's real.

'From the start they hear strong messages about Y'shua, His love and redemption, His resurrection and the new life He offers to all who will commit their lives to Him 100 per cent. We can handle a maximum of eight men in stage one and another seven in stage two. Each stage lasts about six months. When a man reaches the second stage he can go out and work, although he still remains under the supervision of the programme.

'It happens fast – some accept the Lord the same day; but generally within two or three days they accept the Lord and we like to see them baptized with the Holy Spirit within a few weeks. There's no way to get free from drugs and stay free without the power of the Holy Spirit. A drug addict who accepts Y'shua cannot be like a regular churchgoer. A regular churchgoer who doesn't come from an addictive background may be able to get away with compromising their faith, although they would be lukewarm – but these guys can't be like that. They have to be 100 per cent radical for the Lord and filled with the Holy Spirit. We've seen that when these men allow sin into their lives, if they don't repent quickly, they open the door to even more sin and darkness in their lives, and their fall will be rapid. It's either hot or cold with them. They need the power of the Holy Spirit. We all need the power of the Holy Spirit! The Kingdom of God is righteousness, joy and peace in the Holy Spirit. It's not a one-time experience; we need to be filled with the Holy Spirit every day.

'Regarding the men, if any sin comes into their lives – for example, if they are angry with their brother – we live in community here so things are exposed very rapidly – then we deal with it. We can tell whether something is going on or whether they are under spiritual attack. We all pray together. At Beit HaY'shua we have learned to quickly pray for one another. Together we learn the power of prayer. Our walk with the Lord at the centre is very intensive.

'For the first two and a half years, we only took Jews. We were open to receive Arabs but I think God, in His wisdom, waited until we were more mature, and three months ago He brought the first two Arabs into the programme, one from a Muslim background who had been a drug addict for twenty-five years and came to us in a wheelchair, having spent fifteen years in prison. Drugs are readily available in the prisons. The other Arab was from a "Christian background" but his family is a family of criminals. He came to us not knowing how to read or write because from an early age, instead of going to school, he was sent on criminal errands. A drug addict since the age of eleven, he's now thirty-one. The one who came from a Muslim background took about two and a half weeks until he had a breakthrough with the Lord – we actually had to remove him from the programme for about a week because he misbehaved, but we felt it right to take him back. Then he had a breakthrough and stepped forward in a meeting and proclaimed Y'shua as his God, and the Lord gave him major deliverance from evil spirits, filled him with the Holy Spirit, and he's a changed person. The other Arab also had a breakthrough with the Lord and they have both now been baptized in water and baptized in the Holy Spirit, and we see the relationship between them and the Jewish brothers is now very good.

'We teach them that our first identity is as a child of God. We believe God is restoring Israel but that doesn't mean the Arabs don't have a place here. God wants the Arabs to preach the gospel to Jews and Arabs and other nations too. There are no second-class citizens in the family of God. God has a specific purpose for Israel but that doesn't mean the Arabs are left out. So we are helping them all to see they are children of the Most High and that is their most important identity. Whilst we encourage them to love each other, conflicts often arise here. Yesterday there was trouble between one of the Arab brothers and one of the Jewish guys. But there again, some days I have to sort out many conflicts between Jewish brothers!

'We want to see Israelis meet their Messiah and be saved. That is the motivation of my life. I want to see Israelis believing in Y'shua and discipled into becoming servants of the Lord. What we've done here in this centre to date I see as only the beginning. We have a vision for a women's centre. But everything is in the Lord's time. We have the burden but we wait until the Lord brings together the team and the place. Meanwhile we feel we have to get out and bring the good news of Y'shua to our people.

'Last year a core group of us was sent out from

the previous congregation which I pastored. We have established a new congregation called Y'shuat Yisrael (Salvation of Israel) with a vision for outreach, discipleship and community. We are experiencing a wonderful move of the Holy Spirit and the Lord is placing within us a passion and hunger for more of Him. One of the men in our leadership team is an evangelist – and he's organizing evangelistic outreaches. We are beginning to see new believers come into the congregation. The prayer and intercession ministries in the congregation are also developing. Sometimes we have all-night prayer meetings in addition to our usual prayer meetings. We believe that all work for God must be based on prayer. We've also started home groups. We've started a Bible school. It's a community life and we want to grow as a family.

'My understanding of the Scriptures is that as more and more Israelis get saved, the gospel will go out from Israel to all the nations because it says, "What shall their restoration be but life from the dead?" So I envisage a new infusion of spiritual life to go from Israel to the nations of the world. It's already beginning. Three months ago the Lord showed me that for a long time in Israel we've said, "Some day God will visit His people and pour out His Holy Spirit and we'll see revival." I believe the challenge God is giving us is to stop putting off revival to some future date and believe for God to move now! Revival is simply the manifestation of the Kingdom of God in our midst. Revival begins when we commit our lives 100 per cent to the Lord and seek God until we have breakthrough. We're going to repent of anything that needs repenting of and we're going to break through.

'If I can speak about the Messianic Body here in Israel, I think for too long we've relied too much on the prayers of other people around the world, and we don't do enough praying ourselves. We ourselves are not serious enough about God. I know there is a lot of spiritual warfare going on here, but I believe that if we, the local believers, will seek God, He will be found. I believe that at this time God wants to pour out His Holy Spirit, but we need to be very radical. And this begins with the leadership here. Our vision is to meet with God and see the Kingdom of God established.

'God is raising up a commando force of men who will be totally committed and will go wherever the Lord sends them. I can see God sending people from our congregation to other nations. Maybe some of them will start rehab centres in some other nations. There are many needs abroad. I believe God will send us to the down and outs in whatever nation we're in, including our Arab brothers.'

CHAPTER 12

Marcel Rebiai

It was Friday, 7 September 2007. I had been interviewing for seven days without a break, and today it was time to take stock and visit Marcel Rebiai in Jerusalem. Marcel's fascinating life-story – from Algerian Muslim, to European Christian, to Messianic leader in Jerusalem – is told in my earlier book, *Israel: the Mystery of Peace*, published by Authentic Media.

Suffice to say, Marcel is a highly respected leader in the Messianic community both in Israel and beyond, and, amongst other things, is part of a committee which leads a movement called 'Sitting at Y'shua's Feet' which gathers pastors from Israel, both Jewish and Arab, together at regular intervals for times of prayer and discussion. Twice a year they retreat to the desert for two or three days.

Marcel and his Swiss-born wife Regula live in Jerusalem where they run the organization they founded called the Community of Reconciliation; they have teams in France and Switzerland as well as Israel. Their house in Jerusalem overlooks Mount Zion and the view from the roof is incredible! Before lunch Marcel took me up there to see the view. To the left I saw the Mount Zion Hotel; looking straight ahead, across the Hinnom Valley, was the Dormitian Abbey; down the hill and to the right was the Jewish Quarter, and then up to the Mount of Olives; further to the right and in the distance, just in sight, I could see part of the security wall surrounding Bethlehem. It was a panorama that told so many stories.

We sat outside on their veranda and shared lunch together. Members of the Community joined us. It was one of those moments when I couldn't quite believe I was sitting looking at the very spot where Jesus will return and talking to people who believe He could return at any time and whose daily lives reflect a passion to talk about Jesus to both Jewish and Arab people. If ever a situation concentrated the mind it was here, where the location and the people I was with shared a common purpose: they were living for and waiting for the return of the Lord, and in the meantime doing all they could to make Him known.

Marcel had been instrumental in introducing me to many of the people mentioned already in this book; he is a central figure here. So after lunch the others left whilst Marcel and I stayed where we were, under the shade of a leafy tree. He was keen to hear how I had got on with the many interviews I'd recorded so far. We talked about the extraordinary way many of the people I had met had come out of the hippie movement in America, drawn as if by invisible threads to discover their Jewish roots, then discover Y'shua and then feel compelled to move to Israel, only to find themselves working for the salvation of Israel.

I wanted to hear Marcel's perspective on this. What has God been doing these past thirty years or so, and what is the bigger picture? In other words, where is this all going? What is Israel's destiny?

'Let's start with the fact that whatever happens here in Israel, God is the author,' Marcel began. 'Everything that you have heard this week from the people you have met has to do with the redemption and salvation of the nations. We must not forget that the promise given to Abraham was that through his seed all the nations would be blessed. I believe that Y'shua came and made it possible for this to happen. I also believe that Israel is called to be a kingdom of priests. And we know that the place of a priest is to mediate between man and God. A priest brings the heart of God to man; he also brings man to God. We also know that a priest has God's passion in his heart towards man. In Old Testament times a priest had first to bring a sacrifice to purify himself before he could stand before God on behalf of the people. Now Y'shua is the only one who can sanctify and purify the people of Israel, making them fit to be a priestly nation.

'Even though Y'shua was rejected by Israel as a nation, yet there were a few who fulfilled their calling and became "priests" and brought in the "first fruit", both Jews from Israel and Gentiles from the nations. The first fruit are the "Bride of Christ" – those who enjoy an intimate relationship with God. There is nothing more intimate than the relationship between a bridegroom and his bride. What a calling for those who believe they are part of the Bride of Christ and what a prominent place God has given to the Bride of Christ! I believe only those who understand this will be able to be part of God's plan to release Israel into her destiny.

'Paul says, it's not the church who should be jealous of Israel; rather, it's the other way round – Israel should be jealous of the church, jealous that the church is the Bride with an intimate relationship and a passion for the Messiah.

'If this can be understood by the church in the nations, then I believe the church will stop competing with the calling of Israel; she has no need to do that. The church does not release Israel into her calling when she is competitive or tries to gain some selfish advantage. It's manipulative when the church only helps Israel in order to get something for herself. So I believe a church that understands she is the Bride of Christ is deeply secure in her identity. And a church that has an intimate relationship with the Messiah will start to understand His plan for Israel.

'It's a mystery. There is only one Bride. And this Bride is hand-picked from the nations and Israel. I believe the final chapter in history will be the ingathering of a harvest the likes of which have never been seen before, and this ingathering is linked with the restoration of Israel. When the church is really close to the heart of the Lord, they will understand His passion for Israel.

'Many people wonder how the church in the nations connects to what's going on here in Israel. I believe the key to understanding is to understand God's heart. It's not a matter of culture or politics. Do I know the heart of the Bridegroom? If I do, then I will understand His passion, which has to do with the restoration of Israel. There are so many Scriptures that have to do with the restoration of Zion.'

As I looked over towards Mount Zion, Marcel continued: 'As you can see, Mount Zion is an actual place. But when the Bible talks about Zion it's a synonym for two things – Jerusalem and the Jewish people; the two are inseparable because Zion, Jerusalem and the Jewish people are a dwelling-place for God.

'1 Kings 9 talks about what happened after Solomon

finished building the Temple. The Lord said to him, "I have consecrated this temple, which you have built, by putting my Name there forever. My eyes and my heart will always be there."[1] If we take this seriously, we realize that God says He will connect His name forever with Jerusalem – the actual place. Jesus Himself referred to Jerusalem as "the City of the Great King".[2] It's His city and dwelling-place.

'You cannot separate the Jewish people from the land because the calling of the Jews can only be released, developed and take place in connection with the land. In Ezekiel 36 we read how Israel being out of the land was a sign of judgment; the people had to leave the land because they were defiling it by "their conduct and their actions".[4] Then the land was waiting for the return of the people. Isaiah says, "As a young man marries a maiden, so will your sons marry you".[5]

'It's hard for Jews who live in the Diaspora, outside the land of Israel, to hear that if they, as Jews, really want to be part of the fulfilment of their calling, they have to come back. That's what the Word of God says.

'Joel 2:1 also speaks about Zion being the holy mountain of the Lord. Also Psalm 2. We have more verses in Micah 4:1–5. And again in Isaiah 2, which speaks about Zion being the Mountain of the Lord and the place where the Lord is going to gather the nations in the last days. It is here He will challenge their attitude towards the Messiah; this is the place where He will judge the nations; and here He will bring an end to all wars.

'But I believe Zion signifies much more than just giving the Jews their own homeland. It's all about God and His passion and desire to redeem the nations. In Zephaniah 3 we read, "I will remove from this city those who rejoice in their pride. Never again will you be haughty on my holy hill. But I will leave within you the meek and humble, who trust in the name of the Lord."[6]

'We understand from this that God's vision for the Jewish people and for Jerusalem is for the glory of the Messiah to be manifested to all nations from here. That's why Simeon described Jesus as "a light for revelation to the Gentiles and for glory to your people Israel".[7]

'In other words, God is going to transform the nation of Israel, and when this happens the nations will see that there is only one God. The church should therefore be deeply moved and excited about this and should be in prayer that God would have mercy on this nation of Israel; that He will quickly bring them out of the darkness, pride and injustice they are currently living in. The enemy does not want the church to understand this because he knows God's plan concerns the nations – and it's all linked to the Jews!'

As well as projecting into the future and exploring what Israel's destiny is, this book is also about the story so far; in other words, what has led up to the situation as we find it now. So it's about the past, the present and the future. We've heard how, when many of the people in this book came to Israel during the 1960s and 1970s, there were only a handful of Messianic believers in Israel; however, today there are many thousands of believers. I put it to Marcel that one thing these people have in common is that they are all working for the salvation of Israel. Did he agree?

'Yes. The name of Jesus has never been so well known in Israel as it is today and people here are having to deal with this name. They see that Messianic Jews are a reality. The Jewish orthodox community oppose Messianic Jews because they are constantly confronting the nation with this name, Jesus! Hence there is a growing awareness that there is a connection between Jesus and the nation of Israel. In the past they were able to ignore the name of Jesus. Today they can't. I see this as God preparing the soil and bringing people, the first fruit, to the Lord. I also believe God is preparing Israel for the day when, as Zechariah says, "They will look on me, the one they have pierced."[8]

'And when we look at Israeli society today, we see a desperate, disillusioned people. Many are realizing the old Zionist dream hasn't worked because they see both the political and spiritual leaders are corrupt. Consequently they have nobody to turn to for orientation; nothing to believe in. Many Israelis realize this and they are starting to ask themselves, "What are we doing?" which in turn generates a feeling of insecurity.'

Marcel knows the Messianic leaders in Israel well. So, taking this a step further, how would he describe the mood and expectation of the Messianic leadership in Israel today regarding Israel's destiny of being a light to the nations?

'There is a general expectation here that God is about to bring a revival to Israel through the youth that will affect the nation. Why? Because, as I have just mentioned, the people are feeling insecure, so they are more open to listen; they realize neither Rabbinical Judaism nor politics holds the answers. Also, in the past ten years, I have noticed a new boldness amongst Messianic Jews to get out and proclaim the name of Jesus. Today, here in Israel, Messianic Jews are now actively bringing people to the Lord, although the leaders largely came to the Lord through the testimony of non-Jews, when they were living abroad, especially during the 1960s and 1970s.

'There are still a large number of non-Jews who are witnessing to the Jewish community worldwide. But in Israel today, it's hard to find a Christian who is willing to witness to Jews. There are many here who are supporting community projects, but the majority are very hesitant and careful not to offend Jewish people with the gospel. However, those who do witness see people come to the Lord. I think the most important thing Christians can do is to bring the gospel to the Jews and at the same time help and support the Jewish believers in their work. Thank God Messianic Jews increasingly understand the importance of evangelizing their own people and are concentrating on the salvation of Israel.'

'What about the nations and being a light there?' I asked Marcel.

'At the present time, as far as I am aware, I have to admit there are few who have a passion to see the nations coming to know Him. Messianic Jews who are involved outside Israel are mainly involved with teaching the church about her Jewish roots. As for reaching out to the non-believing world, the vision is here, but there are many questions. Who is going to send us? Who is going to help us? I dream that one day we will send out missionaries from within the Jewish people, and the Arab people, to Europe to preach about Jesus.'

I sensed Marcel was holding back on this one, so I put it to him that I found it interesting to hear him say many Messianic leaders spend a lot of their time teaching the church about the place of Israel. Is this a frustration? Does he think the church should have understood this by now? 'Are you being held back by the demands of Christians for more and more teaching?' I asked.

'Precisely. I'm waiting for the moment when Israel

will be released to be a light to the nations; bringing the gospel to the nations. God has promised that: "In those days ten men from all languages and nations will take firm hold of one Jew by the hem of his robe and say, 'Let us go with you, because we have heard that God is with you.'"[9] And this will not be a Rabbinical Jew. This will be somebody who reflects the heart and face of the Messiah. I think the church should help Messianic Jews to be a light to the nations by helping to send them out; they need help and support. If the church in the nations does not wake up and understand God's heart for what is going on here, they may end up dying in their own narrow circle and they will experience Islam becoming a judgment over the church. Islam is going to hate and attack the church anyway. So let us be attacked when we stand in the right place with God's passion.

'There are some in the Gentile church who believe that Israel will be saved and who invest in the Messianic Body and work in harmony. But there are some Gentile Christian organizations who have promised and signed an agreement not to mention the name of Jesus here. This is a tragedy; it is the worst form of anti-Semitism, because if they really believe what is written in the Word of God – "I am not ashamed of the gospel, because it is the power of God for the salvation of everyone who believes: first for the Jew, then for the Gentile"[10] – how can you explain why they have signed such a pact? Is it to avoid conflict and save their own skin? Is it to avoid being attacked and being accused of being like the Nazis and killing Jews? The Jewish community can get very angry because the cross is a scandal to them. So it's quite a challenge to have a love for the Jewish people and also to preach this deeply provocative gospel to them and not to back off.'

Marcel had spoken from his heart and I sensed his anguish. By now I could see more clearly than ever before that believers in Israel are living in a different spiritual time zone to the majority of Christians in the rest of the world. As I left Marcel and Regula that Friday afternoon, all the doubts I had felt about this book the previous day had been well and truly eclipsed as I became more and more convinced about the relevance and importance of the stories I had gathered that week. As I walked up the hill towards the bus stop, I understood that writing this book had to have priority for the next three or four months.

It is now early January 2008. The book is almost complete. There are just two more chapters to write, and as I look back at the order in which the interviews were conducted and the stories were written, I am intrigued to see that the final two stories have huge implications for the future and illustrate perfectly Israel's destiny.

CHAPTER 13

Dan Sered

It was Sunday, 9 September 2007. Sunday is a working day in Israel; the first day of the week. I had spent a quiet *Shabbat* (Saturday) going for a long walk in the morning and reading in the afternoon. Tomorrow I would be flying back to London. With twelve interviews 'in the bag', I had two more to go: one today and the other on my next trip to Israel in three weeks' time.

My time with Marcel Rebiai had been invaluable. He helped me understand how much still has to happen in Israel before she fully realizes her destiny. The stories I was gathering from Jewish believers at this moment in time were revealing where things 'are at' today as well as looking back and charting the rapid growth of the Messianic Jewish movement over the past sixty years and also looking ahead and outlining the vision for the fulfilment of Israel's destiny. Over the past week I had met many pioneers – people who are now getting on in years. However, from what they have been saying, it is clear that the younger generation are picking up the baton and starting to run. How interesting that the first person I met on this trip, Yoel Ben David, and the last person who I was about to meet, are both typical of the next generation: a generation who are prepared to be brave and be seen and heard on the streets and in the media.

Dan Sered is Director of Jews for Jesus in Israel and he's not yet thirty! Leading a team of ten full-time workers, he is in the front line of evangelism in Israel – a Jewish believer who unashamedly talks about Y'shua to Israelis on the streets. His aim? To make the name of Y'shua an unavoidable issue in Israel. That takes courage.

We arranged to meet in Jerusalem outside the Hapoalim Bank in Ben Yehuda Street at 1 p.m. Dan's office is in Tel Aviv, but he was preaching at a Baptist Church in Jerusalem that morning and was ready for lunch! Dan led the way to a restaurant he knew. It was busy. I wondered whether he might be ill at ease about having so many Israeli people within earshot; after all, Jews for Jesus is not the most popular organization in Israel! But I was wrong. Far from being 'careful' with what he was saying, he was completely relaxed. In fact, I would go so far as to say he would have been delighted if the people on the next table had interrupted him at any time.

I wanted to know two things: Why did he get involved with a radical organization like Jews for Jesus, and how will his work affect Israel's destiny? And so we clipped on the mikes, ordered lunch and started to record.

'I was born in 1978 and raised in Herzilya [a northern suburb of Tel Aviv]. I don't think you can get a more typical Israeli home background than mine. Both my parents were born and raised in Romania. They moved to Israel in the sixties and met each other here. My Dad came when he was nineteen and my Mom came when she was sixteen and finished her schooling here. My grandparents escaped to Israel from communist Romania. So my parents grew up under communism and came here with an anti-communist mindset. They became very Israeli and very Zionistic very quickly.

'My Dad became an electrical engineer and then joined the army. He had a long army career and by the time he retired he was a colonel. He fought in the Six Day War and the Yom Kippur War. My mother graduated from the University of Tel Aviv with a degree in Maths and helped develop the high-tech industry here in Israel. She started working in the computer industry when computers were the size of a large room!

'We were a secular family. We celebrated the religious holidays in our own way. We occasionally went to synagogue. We kept *kosher* because everybody did. My parents saw themselves as intellectual people and always told my brother and I that God wasn't real.

'So I grew up in this secular climate where God didn't exist. But I always believed God was real. At school we studied the *Tenach* [the Old Testament] and all the stories convinced me even more that God was real. I looked at the orthodox Jews and wondered whether that's what I ought to become. And I was excited by my Bar Mitzvah at the age of thirteen. At about this time, my school teacher began teaching on the subject of the *Mashiach* [Messiah] because there was a rabbinical movement who claimed one of their rabbis was the Messiah. One of the verses she discussed with us told how the Messiah would come from the tribe of Judah; the teacher told us He hadn't come yet. We studied His lineage and learnt that the Messiah is going to come from the tribe of Judah. Well, I didn't know what tribe I was from, so how would I know whether or not the Messiah, when He came, was from the tribe of Judah? Where are the records? Nobody knows any more.

'I was also studying with a rabbi who was preparing me for my Bar Mitzvah, so I decided to ask him about this. And he looked puzzled. He told me not to worry about it because, he said, when the Messiah comes we will know. But I was keen to know how we would prove that He was from the tribe of Judah. And the rabbi told me again that we would just know. I still believed in God but this didn't make any sense to me. In my mind there were two types of people – Jews and Gentiles. The Jews were either religious or secular, and the Gentiles were either Muslims or Catholics. Well, I didn't want to become a Muslim and I didn't want to become a Catholic. So I felt I had no further options open to me at that time and I certainly had no contact with a Jewish person who believed in Jesus.

'During this time my Dad retired from the army and his new job took us to New York, where he was sent to work on behalf of the Israeli government. We lived in a Jewish area and only mixed with Jewish people. I graduated from high school and started at Stony Brook University in New York where I studied Maths, just like my mother. I needed to earn some money, so started tutoring students who needed some extra help in Maths, which is how I met a girl called Dinah. She was intrigued by my accent and asked if I was Russian. I told her I was an Israeli and that excited her because she was Jewish too.

'So after her Maths class we continued talking, and it was during one of those conversations that Dinah told me she believed in Y'shua. Now you have to understand how amazing this was for me. I had no idea who Y'shua was. I spoke Hebrew and understood that the word Y'shua meant "salvation" – but who was Y'shua? Dinah told me that Y'shua was Jesus' Hebrew name, and I was amazed.

Two things hit me. First of all, to find out that Jesus had a Hebrew name that meant "salvation", and was not called "Yeshu", as I had been taught. And secondly, I was shocked to meet a Jewish person who believed in Jesus. I had no idea such people existed! All this happened on a Friday. We met the following Monday for lunch, and that's when Dinah opened the Old Testament and showed me prophecies that spoke about the Messiah. I remembered what I had learnt in school. Then she turned to the New Testament and showed me how Jesus had fulfilled those prophecies. And I believed it immediately.

'However, I was worried about what my parents would say. Dinah warned me they probably wouldn't like it. This all happened on 5 December 1997, when I was nineteen years old. I told Dinah I would not dedicate my life to Jesus until I had told my parents, and it took me a week to find enough nerve. In the meantime Dinah and her family, who are also believers, were praying. A week later I went to my parents and told them I believed Jesus was the Messiah, and a miracle happened. They laughed at me and told me this was my way of rebelling and I would grow out of it. That was great! I was able to stay living at home.

'The next day I went to Dinah and told her I believed and that's when I officially gave my life to the Lord. For three months everything at home was peaceful; my parents would mock me occasionally but it was light-hearted and life carried on as usual. However, after three months they realized this was no passing phase and they thought I was sacrificing too much for my faith. For example, I used to love basketball and watched it every Sunday on TV. But now I was going to church instead. In addition, every Friday I went to the Jews for Jesus

service in Manhattan. This was too much for my parents.
They sent me to an anti-missionary rabbi. They accused
me of being brainwashed and sent me to a psychiatrist.
They put many restrictions on my life, and since I was still
living at home, I had no choice but to leave. For years this
put a great strain on our relationship, which previously
had been close.

'In August 1999 I married Dinah. In December
1999 I graduated from university and started training
to be a missionary with Jews for Jesus in New York. In
August 2000 Dinah and I moved back to Israel and today
we have three children. My parents started having a
relationship with us again on 1 December 2000, the day
our first daughter was born.

'During our first six months in Israel, I finished
my missionary training. In September 2000 our Jews
for Jesus ministry got an official non-profit status in
Israel. Now that we were an official non-profit-making
organization, it was time for the team to put on the Jews
for Jesus T-shirts!

'For five years I had the privilege of leading
campaigns. The first campaign that I led was in Atlanta,
and the last was in New York. All were part of an operation
called "Behold Your God".[1] The thing that always excited
me about these campaigns was that David Brickner,
Executive Director of Jews for Jesus, saw them as just
the first stage; the second stage would be a "Behold Your
God" campaign in Israel itself! So I always had that in the
back of my mind, and I know that's why David gave me a
lot of experience in leading campaigns.

'David Brickner came to meet the team here in Israel
and said, "Look, most of you are *Sabra* [locally born]. I
want you guys to begin to pray and begin to lay down the

foundations for 'Behold Your God Israel'." He challenged our local team and said, "You guys are the experts. This is your country, this is where you live. Come up with the vision – we'll bring it to the leadership of Jews for Jesus and see if it will be accepted." So we had been thinking about this for a couple of years. Then a year ago, I was appointed the leader here in Israel.

'We came up with one vision... then another... and finally, in December 2006, our third vision was adopted by the Jews for Jesus leadership. We needed their blessing because we need the help of the entire organization to pull it off. Not just the entire organization – we need the Body of Christ all over the world to help us out, including the local Body here in Israel.

'The land of Israel has twelve distinct geographical areas and they have names like Gush Dan, which is the greater Tel Aviv area. We decided to conduct an evangelistic campaign in each of these areas over the next six years – so two campaigns a year. We identified that the best times of the year to conduct these campaigns are during the spring and during the autumn. In the winter it rains too much (God willing!) and in the summer it's way too hot. We're starting in 2008 and will carry on until 2013, unless Jesus comes back.'

'Surely the first campaign is going to attract so much media interest that the whole country will hear about it,' I said.

'That's our prayer. We will start in the area we're most familiar with – the Gush Dan area – in May 2008. We'll take billboards and we'll advertise and we know it will create a buzz all over the country – which is what we want to do because we want to make Jesus, Y'shua, an unavoidable issue to our people here in Israel. Most people in the land don't even know Y'shua's real name – they call Him "Yeshu" (which is a derogatory name). We hope that by the end, with God's grace, they'll at least know His real name!'

'How are you going to go about it?'

'We'll be out on the streets wearing our T-shirts and handing out tracts. We'll engage with the media. We'll call people on the telephone. We'll go door to door. We want half of each team to be Hebrew speaking and half to be English speaking because so many Israelis speak English. We have done some research which shows that English speakers are very effective when talking to Israelis on the streets because they sometimes find it intimidating when spoken to by a fellow Israeli in Hebrew about such a controversial subject. But they are willing to speak to English speakers and Gentiles. So we're going to use both!'

'Are you going to involve Arab Christians?'

'Yes. In the Upper Galilee we want our team to be half Hebrew speaking and half Arab speaking because we know there are a lot of Arabic speakers there.'

I was interested to hear that Dan wanted to include English-speaking Gentiles in these campaigns; but don't Jewish people have a problem historically with the Christian world?

'Yes, but they tolerate Christians and realize they are important because they want Christian tourism. So when a Christian approaches a Jewish person on the streets, they immediately think they're a tourist. Somebody who might not listen to me will listen to you because you're a tourist and you're doing what Christians are supposed to do!'

'That might work with a secular mindset, but what

about the religious people?' I asked.

'You've spoken to Yoel; a foreigner shared the gospel with him and I've heard other, similar testimonies. But above all, it's biblical, because the Apostle Paul told the Gentiles it was their job to provoke the Jews to jealousy; and I think he meant that literally. It's not something we came up with – it's the Apostle Paul's strategy!'

'What are you anticipating will be the response?'

'We know we're going to face a lot of opposition. We've just conducted a week-long probe campaign in Tel Aviv, and we found people turned very angry, even violent, when we talked to them about Y'shua. We know people will try to stop us by accusing us of acting illegally. But it's very important to remember that in Israel today there is no law that forbids evangelism; rather, this country allows freedom of speech. There is one law that states you're not allowed to evangelize or to share with a minor – that's anybody under the age of eighteen – a religion that's contrary to what his parents believe. But in Jews for Jesus we always take the principle that we don't share the gospel with minors. There is another law that states you're not allowed to entice anybody to believe in your religion by paying them or giving them gifts, which we don't do anyway. So our methodology is totally legal. If we have to fight in the courts, we have lawyers and we are ready to do that. We may even get some hostility from the government. We are thinking about all these scenarios. At the same time we know this is the time to run these campaigns. We've seen an openness in Israel. There's a hunger for it. If we don't do it now, then when? After all, one day all Israel will be saved – that's our hope. Jesus said, "I tell you the truth, you will not finish going through the cities of Israel before the Son of Man comes."[2]

Maybe we are playing a small part in His plan.'

'You've made it very clear that the Gentile church has a responsibility to share this job with you.'

'Yes, I don't know whether the time of the Gentiles has come or not, but I do believe the Apostle Paul makes it clear that the Gentiles have a responsibility to bring the gospel back to Israel. Israel is an amazing country. We get so many Christian tourists here every year, but so few of them come and do missionary work. The church goes all over the world on mission trips, but they only come as tourists to Israel. I don't understand it! I'm all for tourism, but why not do some missionary work while you're here?

'The nations are so concerned about peace in the Middle East, but I think they are missing the point. There isn't going to be peace in the Middle East. If anybody wants to bless Israel, they need to bring the gospel to Israel. Millions of Christians come here every year. If they did three days of evangelism as part of their trip, Israel would not be so unreached with the gospel.

'And yet the fact stands that Israel has been unreached with the gospel. Most Israelis have not heard about Y'shua. That's exactly the reason we're doing the campaign, because we want to change that. To get fruit, you have to sow a lot of seeds. The seeds haven't been sown here. So we're going to start sowing a lot of seeds. Once we reach Israel with the gospel, maybe then Israel can fulfil her destiny. Right now, how can Israel fulfil her destiny of being "a light to the nations" when she is in darkness? Israel is in unbelief and that is why it is so important for the church to reach out and to bring the gospel to the nation of Israel. If not now, then when?'

And what will the effect of that be?, I wondered. There

was no doubt in my mind that Dan believes, as did Yoel Ben David, that now is the time for Israel to be told that Y'shua is the Messiah. The last time Israel heard this message was 2,000 years ago. In the intervening years, since AD 70, Jewish people have been living outside of Israel. Since 1948 the Jewish people have again had a land to call their own and have been returning to live there from all over world. For the first time since then, Jewish believers will be taking the gospel to their own people in their own land. One can only wonder at the effect this will have on Israel realizing her destiny.

CHAPTER 14

Rita Tsukahira

I had planned to meet Rita Tsukahira during September; but it proved impossible. I wanted so much to include her story in this book and feared the opportunity was lost. However, whilst I was back in Israel with a group in early October, Rita was able to come to our hotel in Jerusalem, and there we recorded this interview.

Why is Rita's story important in the context of Israel's destiny? This was a question Rita had asked herself for many years. Her husband Peter is one of the leaders of Kehilat HaCarmel alongside David Davis. He is a distinguished Bible teacher and writer and travels widely. Rita is Jewish; the story of her life began in New York. Her husband comes from a Japanese background. As Rita's story unfolds, it reveals a woman who has wanted to find the particular calling God has had for her. She has been around men and woman who have become well known in the Messianic Jewish world. Indeed, Rita has helped them to achieve their goals. Meanwhile, she remained in the background wondering when God would open the door for her to use the gifts He'd given her.

Events taking place over the past couple of years have shown that now is that time. Due to the deterioration of the political situation in Sudan, and through a series of unexpected events that Rita would never have dreamt possible, she now finds herself running a shelter for Sudanese refugees (many of whom are Muslim) on Mount Carmel in northern Israel, where she lives. These people, fearing for their lives, have fled the recent fighting in Sudan and sought refuge in Israel, entering the country via Egypt. And, as Rita later explains, these are a people whom it would have been impossible to reach unless they had fled their country and come to Israel.

And so, after dinner that night, Rita sat down with our group. She had driven up to Jerusalem from Haifa earlier in the day – that's a two- or three-hour drive. After visiting a number of people in Jerusalem, she reached our hotel by 8 p.m. It had already been a long and gruelling day for her and she was planning to drive back home that night. Nevertheless, full of enthusiasm and quite unperturbed at the prospect of not seeing her bed until 1 a.m., she began telling her story.

'My grandparents arrived in America from Eastern Europe and lived in New York, where there is a large Jewish community, so I grew up with a definite Jewish identity. We kept all the holidays and the local synagogue was the focus of my parents' lives. I grew up in the 1950s when memories of the Holocaust were still very strong. There was much talk of Israel and every week in our religious school, a collection was taken to help the needy Jews who had gone to live there. We were quite happy to give some money, but we certainly did not want to go and live in Israel. American Jews were becoming very prosperous and the prospect of giving up so much to move to Israel was not an attractive option to most people.

'However, as I became a teenager, I felt restless and like so many of my generation, I became a hippie. I went to Woodstock, the "definitive event" of our generation. We were determined that we were going to be different from our parents; we were going to create the "new order". I became deeply committed to the political as well as the spiritual desire for something new and, like many others, my search took me into New Age philosophy and the world of drugs. I went to Tufts University near Boston in 1969, which is where I met my husband, Peter, who was also rebelling against our society and culture.

'During that time one of our closest friends killed himself. His name was John. We'd often sat with him when, overwhelmed with feelings of hopelessness and despair, he'd discussed ways in which he could kill himself. We tried to comfort him. We told him there must be "somebody" out there who could help him. But at that time we didn't know who "He" was and sadly, we didn't know where to look for Him.

'John took his life in February 1973. His funeral was held in a Catholic church and, being Jewish, I had never been to a church service before. I had also never heard verses from the New Testament, so when the priest read from the Gospel of John, "Greater love has no one than this, that he lay down his life for his friends",[1] I realized that if Peter and I had known this truth, we could have helped John. But we also knew that we didn't have the courage or love to have laid down our *own* lives.

'As we said our goodbyes to John, those words stayed with us. And that really was what drove Peter and I into a place where we wanted to become new people.

'During that year I experienced a lot of death – of people I knew – and death within me as I experienced the murder of abortion. It was also to be the year of my salvation.

'Peter and I had moved to Santa Fe in New Mexico where many hippies lived – Eitan Shishkoff and his group lived nearby. It was Yom Kippur [October] of 1973 and for some reason, which I didn't understand, I felt very strongly that I needed to be in the synagogue. So I hitch-hiked there in my hippie clothes and during the service somebody came running into the middle of the building shouting, "They've just bombed us!" We immediately knew it was Israel that had been bombed – the Yom Kippur War had begun. For the first time in my life, I felt a strong and genuine tie to Israel. I fasted that day, as is the tradition, and I cried out to God saying, "If you're real, please show me who you are." I was twenty-one years old and had never heard that the Bible was true and that Y'shua was the Messiah for the Jewish people.

'A few weeks later, while we were still living in New Mexico, I was standing by the side of the road hitch-hiking and thinking how nice it would be if a woman stopped to pick me up rather than a man. Ten seconds later a Volkswagen pulled over with two bumper-stickers which read, "Guess who's coming again" and "Christ died for your sins". I got in the car and said to this woman, "Is He really coming again?" She reminded me how, in 1967 during the Six Day War, Jerusalem, which had been in the hands of the Gentiles, was captured and was now in the hands of the Jews. She told me how this related to Jeremiah and other prophecies in the Bible and asked if she could pray with me. I turned to her and said, "But I'm a Jew." When she stopped the car she took my hand and she prayed a very simple prayer: "God, show yourself." Then she dropped me off, but I just knew something profound had happened in that car. A few days later she stopped by with some books and an invitation to visit a coffee house named "Shalom".

'So I went to a meeting there one night and a group of hippies were visiting – most of them were Jewish believers. Eitan Shishkoff got up to speak and I saw something in him that reminded me of our friend John. Eitan had also become a believer through the death of one of his friends. I looked at my watch. I was supposed to meet Peter in a nearby hotel and I knew he'd be waiting for me. But I was compelled to stay in that room. Eitan spoke for a long time and I listened intently. When he'd finished speaking, they all started singing a song: "I have decided to follow Jesus… no turning back." I had never heard anything like it in my life. It was so real, and I felt like the Lord was saying to me, "If you go this way there is no turning back." Now, I had met gurus and people who claimed to have had profound spiritual experiences, but that night God in His mercy showed me the truth.

'Later that evening I returned to the little wooden hut where we were living. Peter was there. He looked at me and said, "You're different." And I told him I had met Y'shua! "Oh, why that?" he said, clearly disappointed, as he had been raised in a church which had no reality or understanding of a living God.

'After a few weeks I went back to New York for a short period while Peter stayed on in New Mexico. I told my parents about my new faith and they were very upset, as I had expected them to be. In the meantime Peter also was convinced that the Bible was true and Y'shua was calling him. Six months later we were married. My parents refused to come to our wedding because it was in a church. They were deeply offended and my father told me that it was like I was "dead" to them; it was a very painful time for both me and my family.

'However, we went ahead with our plans, as the Lord

had given Peter a vision that all four parents would be standing with us at our wedding, reading the Scriptures, two on each side. But the wedding took place and only his mother came. Where was the vision? I share that with you because, though the vision may not happen when we think it will, God will bring it to pass – if He promises. And He did! A year to the day later, six months after our marriage, all four parents stood with us, reading from the Proverbs and the Psalms (by this time Peter and I were in a Bible Institute in Dallas, Texas).

Shortly after our wedding, the Lord had told Peter that we would live in Japan before going to live in Israel. And that's exactly how He led us.

'The period in Japan was interesting because it was a training time. God gave us both "professions", so to speak. Mine was teaching communication theory in a university and Peter was a marketing manager in the high-tech industry. At the same time he was helping to lead an international congregation in the centre of Tokyo.

'In 1987 we knew that the Lord was saying it was time to move to Israel. Through a series of divine appointments, Peter was offered a job in Haifa in northern Israel as well as one in Tel Aviv. We knew a few Israeli believers and someone we respected advised us, "If you want to be with the other believers, go to Tel Aviv, but if you want to start something for God, go to Haifa." And so we went to Haifa.

'It was a hard three years, and we wondered what the Lord was saying to us. In December 1990 Peter was offered the chance to go to the States to represent an Israeli company. We really sought God about what to do. We'd been in Haifa for three years but hadn't found the right people to "partner with" to begin any work for the Lord. We thought that maybe it was time to leave. One morning, a week before the Gulf War started on 17 January 1991, we stayed at home to pray and seek God's will. We knew Saddam was threatening to obliterate half of Israel, so we felt the pressure! Our son was one year old and our daughter was four. As we were praying, the Lord took us to John 12, where it says that unless a grain of wheat falls into the ground and dies, there can be no fruit, and that if we try to save our lives, we lose them, but if we give our lives for the sake of the Lord, we will truly live. Then we knew we were here to stay. We also wondered if God was preparing us to die in the coming Gulf War!

'It was at this time that we met David and Karen Davis. They had come to Israel the year before from New York and were working with drug addicts, both Jews and Arabs – a pioneering "One New Man" ministry. David saw in Peter a man he could work with and as we began to pray with them, the Lord indicated that we were to start a congregation. He led us to the top of Mount Carmel to a place called Stella Carmel where we rented a small chapel for very little money.

'The congregation soon began to grow and we needed more space. Eventually we were given an unused piece of land by the owners of Stella Carmel, and we built a worship centre there which was opened in 1998. Five hundred people from forty nations helped us complete it. It was truly a "one new man" work!

'Now I want to share something very personal. I had come from Japan, where I was teaching in a prestigious university. Peter and I were leading productive lives and were seeing young people coming to the Lord. Then we came to Israel and "died", so to speak, for those three years before the Lord indicated what he wanted us to do. Then Peter, who has an anointing as a teacher, found a place alongside David Davis. Karen Davis, who is an immensely gifted singer and worship leader, was fulfilling her role and others came to help build our congregation – all with various gifts. But I kept asking God what I was meant to do. For a long time this bothered me. I knew that God had given me relationships with a number of Israeli women, and I was able to pray for them and encourage them to come to the congregation on *Shabbat*, and also to help them in small ways; but that didn't feel like a real calling. I felt like the odd one out; the one without a clear mandate from the Lord.

'In 2002 the congregation purchased the two Stella Carmel buildings. It was then I heard the Lord saying we should use the smaller one, called The Annexe, to start a refuge, a shelter for women. I'd never done anything like that before. So, we cleaned the building and made it comfortable, and gradually and quietly – we never advertised – women who were victims of domestic violence heard about us. Some were Israeli Jews, some were Arabs, some were migrant workers. Somehow they heard there was a place to help them and came knocking on our door.

'One day in March 2006, I received a phone call from the immigration police saying, "We've heard about your shelter. Could you take in a Sudanese woman? She's at an army base on the Egyptian border and has a little daughter." They didn't tell me she was pregnant! When I put the phone down the Lord said – and I had never heard His voice speaking to me so clearly before – "This is going to be big." I knew there were problems in Sudan and had heard that refugees were arriving at the border between Egypt and Israel – but in those early days, we had no idea just how many people would be involved.

'What was Israel to do with these refugees? At first the men were put into prison, as they were considered "illegal infiltrators from an enemy state", but the Israeli army and immigration police didn't know what to do with the women and children. So they started sending them to me.

'When the first Sudanese mother and her child arrived, we gave her a lovely meal of chicken but she didn't eat it because it was Lent – I didn't know about these things and had no idea there were Catholic Sudanese! Soon after, another Sudanese girl came to us. Nineteen years old and a Muslim, she had been a university campus activist and had been imprisoned and beaten in Sudan for trying to bring Christians and Muslims together for dialogue. Her father was a businessman and she came from a wealthy family. She too was married and she was pregnant. When she heard that an *imam* had issued a death warrant on her life, she fled Sudan and went to Egypt, where she hid for three months.

'Along with other Sudanese asylum seekers, she managed to cross into Israel by paying some Bedouins who brought her to the border at night. However, they were quickly spotted by a group of Israeli soldiers out on patrol, who took them into custody. One of these women told me how scared they were about coming into Israel. They feared the Egyptian soldiers and knew they would be shot if they were found there. They didn't know what to expect from the Israeli soldiers; after all, Sudan is an enemy state in Israel's eyes. To their complete surprise, the Israeli soldiers gave pretzels and juice to their children and treated them kindly.

207

'The Muslim girl had her baby by caesarean section in Beer Sheva and, after a few days, she was sent to us, arriving late at night. Then came another Muslim woman with her small son. Her husband was from an influential family and had been asked to spy for the government – something he refused to do. So they fled to Egypt where their lives also became difficult. Seeing that again and again he was being treated unjustly by his fellow Muslims, he decided to read the New Testament while in the Israeli prison. After his release, he came to me like a Nicodemus, and said that he wanted to know whether Y'shua had really given his life for him. After a number of weeks of study and genuine questions, he made a decision to put his faith in "Yasua" (Y'shua's Arab name), the Messiah for all people.

'Women continued to come from southern Sudan where they were Christians, and others came from Darfur where they are Muslims, and they all lived together in the shelter. Then came the war with Lebanon in July 2006. Ironically, these refugees who were fleeing war, genocide and murder in Sudan found themselves in northern Israel under fire from another radical Islamic group, the Hezbollah.

'After the war, more women and children came and eventually we had twenty-six children and fifteen women living together, while their husbands were in prison. Sadly, on some days violence erupted between the women as hatred and enmity from their pasts surfaced. It wasn't easy but we saw the power of God moving among us, as Muslims came to faith and nominal Christians were delivered of demonic influences from their pasts.

'For almost a year, the Lord told me not to give any interviews to the press. In December 2006 I was given an award by a secular humanitarian group and at that point we felt we could begin to speak to the journalists who were knocking on our door, including Israeli national television. It was a wonderful opportunity to share why we, as Messianic Jews, working alongside Arab believers on our staff, were taking care of refugees – something no one else was doing at that time.

'Today the situation has changed again and hundreds of refugees from Sudan, the Ivory coast and Eritrea are pouring over our borders. We have seen the answer to our prayers that other believers all over the country would become involved with helping them. Most of the Sudanese women who lived with us in that first year have been reunited with their husbands, and homes have been found for them. We are still taking in women – both single and married, usually pregnant – and their children; their husbands are still in prison or in Egypt. Looking back at all that has happened, I am amazed at the incredible opportunity the Lord gave us to show His love and live out what He commands in the *Torah*: "When an alien lives with you in your land, do not mistreat him. The alien living with you must be treated as one of your native-born. Love him as yourself, for you were aliens in Egypt."[2]

'What has this to do with Israel's destiny? Israel is at a place in history where we know many in other nations are turning against us, and what we do within our own borders is crucial. But we must not walk in fear – we have to answer only to the living God. That, I believe, is why we have to obey the Scriptures and not play political games. We could never have imagined God would bring these Sudanese people, through Egypt, to Israel to impact their lives with the gospel. But that is exactly what has happened. All the Sudanese families we have cared for have heard about Y'shua and many of them now believe in Him. The Muslim Sudanese would probably never have heard the gospel unless they had come to Israel. Is that prophetic? I believe so. We read about a highway coming from Egypt to Israel in Isaiah:

> In that day there will be a highway from
> Egypt to Assyria. The Assyrians will go
> to Egypt and the Egyptians to Assyria.
> The Egyptians and Assyrians will worship
> together. In that day Israel will be the third,
> along with Egypt and Assyria, a blessing
> on the earth. The Lord almighty will bless
> them, saying, 'Blessed be Egypt my people,
> Assyria my handiwork, and Israel my
> inheritance.'[3]

By now it was very late, our people were longing to get to bed and Rita had yet to drive home. But how appropriate her story is to this book, and how fitting that hers should be the final story in a book that set out to explore Israel's destiny. This story of Messianic Jewish believers in Israel touching the lives of Muslim people from a hostile neighbouring country and telling them about Jesus surely indicates that God will not be thwarted by the politics of the region; Israel will fulfil her destiny in being a light to the nations!

=====

Afterword

Now that you have reached the end of the book (unless you are one of those people who reads the final chapter first), I would like you to know that one night, midway through my time in Israel gathering these stories, I was overwhelmed by doubt and for a few hours came to think that the entire project was doomed to failure.

It had been a suffocating night when confusion entered my mind and dragged me down to the point of despair. During those dark hours, as I thought about the people I'd met, I was unable to see the threads of similarity running through their stories – truths that would provide the reader with a prophetic insight into the mysterious things that God is doing quietly yet deliberately in the lives of some of His key workers in the land in order for Israel to fulfil her destiny. I was ready to fly home and admit to my publisher that I had made a big mistake in imagining I could complete a book of such magnitude.

But as morning follows night, so hope follows despair. It so happened that I had a few hours free before meeting Zvi Randelman at lunchtime; enough time to go into Jerusalem to buy a book to read over the weekend (it was *Shabbat*) and also a *Jerusalem Post* newspaper. I also prayed that by noontime God would show me something so profound and wise that it would dispel the doubt and confusion in my mind so that I could see the way forward and have the desire and motivation to carry on and finish this book.

Taking the No 7 bus from Ramat Rachel I decided to visit the bookshop at Christ Church by the Jaffa Gate, so I got off the bus at the junction with King George Street close to Montifiore's Windmill. This bizarre structure was built in 1857 by Sir Moses Montifiore who was keen to find a way for poor Jews to support themselves rather than be dependent on donations from wealthy Jews living abroad. The idea was that this windmill would provide an ultra modern method of grinding grain into flour. How well it worked is apparently open to debate!

However, it stands there today as a monument to a man who cared deeply for Jerusalem and her impoverished inhabitants. At the base of the windmill, protected behind plate glass, is a replica of the horse drawn carriage Sir Moses Montifiore and his wife used to ride around 'Palestine'. After the original had been virtually destroyed by fire, the remnants were incorporated into this new carriage. As I looked, I saw a parallel between that carriage and the Jewish people; a remnant who survived the fire of the Holocaust, who came to the land of Israel where God Himself is rebuilding them into a nation who will know Him.

Continuing on my walk I followed the steps down the hill through Yemin Moshe – today an artists' quarter, a beautiful collection of buildings also built by Sir Moses Montifiore – and on the way passed a pomegranate tree. I made a mental note to take a photograph on the way back.

After entering the Old City through the Jaffa Gate I went to the Christ Church bookshop and whilst looking for something to read overheard a conversation between the bookshop manager and an American lady. They were talking about Joseph and how his brothers didn't recognize him when they went down to Egypt to buy grain, even though he was their own flesh and blood; a parallel between the Jewish people of today and their Messiah, Y'shua, whom they don't all recognise yet.

With this thought I left the bookshop and after stopping for a cold drink in Christ Church – it was close to midday and extremely hot – I started to retrace my steps and arrived back at the pomegranate tree.

On closer inspection I noticed that the intense heat from the sun had ripened the pomegranates to the point where their thick skin had dried and, as a consequence, could no longer contain the mature juicy seeds within and had burst open, thereby releasing the seeds that were falling onto the soil where they were able to start a new life!

Never having seen this before, I found myself transfixed as I remembered something I had once been told by a secular Jewish guide when he explained that to an orthodox Jew, the pomegranate represents the *Torah*, the Mosaic Law, and each seed represents a law; the total number of seeds in a pomegranate equates to the number of laws in the *Torah* – 613.

As I stood there looking at the pomegranate tree and the ripe fruit and the seeds, all the confusion and doubts of the night before disappeared. Now I saw Y'shua as the Son (sun). The Law (pomegranate seeds) hidden in the *Torah* (pomegranate) was being released (fulfilled) after much exposure to the Son (sun). The old life, no longer able to contain itself, had burst open, releasing the new life within.

And that was when I realized that the stories I had been listening to all week were of life from the dead; at first so few believers in Israel, but now so many, and the numbers are growing fast. Through the interviews I was collecting during that two week period, I was gathering evidence that something is going on that will soon become apparent; Israel's new disciples are emerging!

Still wanting to buy a book, and the *Jerusalem Post*, yet unable to find a newsagent (such places do not exist in Jerusalem like they do in London!) I remembered that in the King David Hotel there is a shop. It was only a short detour and energised by the revelation of the pomegranate tree I walked into the hotel and went down the stairs to the gift shop. There were many interesting books to choose from and I ended up buying a novel by the Jewish writer, Elie Wiesel. And yes, there was a *Jerusalem Post* too! Then as I turned to pay, my eyes lighted on some pottery pomegranates. I took a closer look, only to find the potter (who I later learned was an orthodox Jew) had shaped the clay to show how the skin of an extremely ripe pomegranate splits open to reveal the seeds inside! And so, to remember this experience, this revelation, I bought one of those handmade pottery pomegranates and during the writing of this book it has sat on my kitchen windowsill – a daily reminder of the prophetic theme running through this book.

I share this personal experience of doubt and vulnerability because it can sometimes seem that stories are gathered and books written in an almost mechanical way. Since that experience I have always believed that this book was special and I do not use the word 'prophetic' lightly.

As the 'parable' of the pomegranate tree shows, Israel's new disciples are an emerging story. Gradually new life is coming out of the old. But there is no contradiction here – rather it is a natural progression. There would be no 'new' if it were not for the 'old'.

The fourteen Messianic Jewish believers whose stories are contained within the covers of this book have explained their understanding of what God is doing in and through them, and the other 10,000 plus like them, in Israel today. If their stories are prophetic and we are now watching Israel completing the fulfilment of her God given destiny – she has returned to the land, been restored as a nation and is now being spiritually revived in order to be a light to the nations – then what is to be the response of the church in the nations?

As somebody once said to me, God is God! If he chooses to make Himself known to the rest of the world through one nation, the people of Israel, who are we to argue?

And so to conclude this book it seems fitting to return to where we started with the quotation from Avi Snyder (European Director of Jews for Jesus).

> If you love Israel and the Jewish people,
> then understand we were chosen to be a
> light to the nations. The best way for the
> church to interfere with the process of
> world evangelization is to keep the gospel
> away from us Jews and not to pray for the
> salvation of Israel and not to pray for the
> people who bring the gospel to the Jewish
> people and believe the lie that Jews don't
> need Jesus (Y'shua) to be saved. But give

us the gospel and pray for the salvation of
Israel and pray for those of us who bring
the gospel to our people and we'll bring the
gospel to everybody we meet because that's
why we were created!

Notes

Introduction
1. Isaiah 49:6; Acts 13:47.

Chapter 1
1. Isaiah 6:9–10.

Chapter 2
1. Romans 1:16.
2. Zechariah 12:10.
3. Romans 11:11.
4. Romans 11:12, 15.
5. Isaiah 2:2–3.
6. Zechariah 8:22.
7. Zechariah 2:10b, 11.
8. Genesis 12:3.
9. Isaiah 49:6.
10. Genesis 12:3.
11. Zechariah 8:23.
12. Ezekiel 36:24–27.

Chapter 3
1. Isaiah 49:6.

2. Ephesians 2:15.
3. Romans 10:1.
4. Romans 11:15.
5. Isaiah 2:3.

Chapter 4

1. Romans 11:15.
2. Zechariah 8:23.
3. Isaiah 49:6; Acts 13:47.
4. Isaiah 27:6.

Chapter 5

1. Luke 24:27.
2. Numbers 21:9.
3. Matthew 16:5–12.
4. Acts 15.
5. Ezekiel 36:22–23.
6. Ezekiel 36:24.
7. Zechariah 12:1–9.
8. Zechariah 14:1–2.
9. Zechariah 14:3–5.
10. Jeremiah 30:7.
11. Zechariah 13:8–9.
12. Zechariah 12:10–14.
13. Ezekiel 38:15–16.
14. Ezekiel 38:21–23.
15. Ezekiel 36:22–23; 28:16, 23; 39:7, 22–23.
16. Zechariah 12:1–3.
17. Zechariah 14:1–2.
18. Luke 12:48.
19. Matthew 23:37–39.
20. Matthew 24:27.
21. Zechariah 12:10.

22. Luke 11:2.
23. Romans 11:18.
24. Romans 11:21.
25. Revelation 3:14–22.
26. Revelation 3:18–19.
27. Zechariah 8:23; 2:11; Ephesians 2:11–22.
28. Matthew 10:23.

Chapter 6
1. Genesis 12:1.

Chapter 7
1. Isaiah 6:9.

Chapter 8
1. 2 Peter 2:21.
2. Ephesians 2:14–16.

Chapter 10
1. Jeremiah 30:18.
2. Isaiah 60:3.
3. Isaiah 60:10.
4. Isaiah 61:5.
5. Joel 2:17.
6. Matthew 23:39.

Chapter 12
1. 1 Kings 9:3.
2. Matthew 5:35.
3. Ezekiel 36:17.
4. Isaiah 62:5.
5. Zephaniah 3:11–12.
6. Luke 2:32.

7. Zechariah 12:10.

8. Zechariah 8:23.

9. Romans 1:16.

Chapter 13

1. The 'Behold Your God' campaigns took the gospel to
every city in the world where 25,000 or more Jews lived.

2. Matthew 10:23.

Chapter 14

1. John 15:13.

2. Leviticus 19:33–34.

3. Isaiah 19:23–25.